Transfer Pricing in
International Business

Transfer Pricing in International Business

A Management Tool for Adding Value

Geoff Turner

First published in 2013 by
Business Expert Press, LLC
222 East 46th Street, New York, NY 10017
www.businessexpertpress.com

ISBN-13: 978-1-60649-348-9 (paperback)

ISBN-13: 978-1-60649-349-6 (e-book)

Business Expert Press International Business collection

Collection ISSN: 1948-2752 (print)
Collection ISSN: 1948-2760 (electronic)

Cover and interior design by Exeter Premedia Services Private Ltd., Chennai, India

First edition: 2013

10 9 8 7 6 5 4 3 2 1

Printed in the United States of America.

Abstract

Trade is understood to have taken place throughout much of recorded history. From those early beginnings, and through all the stumbling blocks, mistakes, and moments of inspiration over the centuries, the development of trade has contributed to the modern, globalized world in which we live. The increasing economic, social, and political importance of trade spawned a phenomenon called the multinational organization.

These organizations are capable of exercising extreme power not only in individual countries but globally for they are a source of revenue, employment, and economic activity. However, these organizations have a national home where profits will ultimately have to come, and in their effort to maximize the amount repatriated, they often engage in internal-pricing practices, known more commonly as transfer pricing, which enrage either their host or home countries, provoking them to monitor and capriciously modify transfer prices as a way of protecting their national income.

These events often create an intense discord that causes managers to take their eye off the reason they are in business in the first place. Transfer pricing is not simply about maximizing income. It is a much more important strategic management issue that, treated unwisely or with ignorance, is likely to lead to an incongruity in the added value of an organization's products and services as well as its crucial return on capital employed.

This book seeks to remind managers of those important issues and how easy it is to create friction between all of the interested parties if the transfer pricing process is not properly thought out. It goes on to provide an insight into how such conflicts can be assuaged or avoided altogether and explains how transfer pricing may become a managerial tool by establishing a common language that may be used as one driver for creating added value throughout the organization.

Keywords

added value, conflict of interest, costs, economic activity, government revenue, multinational organizations, performance measurement, pricing, profit, revenue, risk and return, stakeholders, trade, transfer pricing

Contents

Preface

In an ever-changing global economy, transfer pricing has emerged as a key management issue for multinational organizations. Used effectively, it is an important contributor to enhanced shareholder value. Managing transfer-pricing activities remains critical in an increasingly aggressive business and regulatory environment. Internationally, regulators are expanding their focus on transfer pricing and are currently considering penalties and tax adjustments which, in aggregate, will amount to billions of dollars.

In the future, the managers of any organization engaging in internal cross-border trade will not only face regular intensive investigation of their transfer pricing activities from regulators in many, if not all, of the countries in which they operate, but they will also face scrutiny from their shareholders on the strategic decisions they have taken in managing their transfer pricing activity. This ever-increasing oversight comes as a result of the extraordinary growth in world trade over the last century.

Yet, trade is understood to have taken place throughout much of recorded history. From the time of the ancient Greeks, trade has been conducted between different communities contributing to the development of civilization. From those early beginnings, and through all the stumbling blocks, mistakes, and moments of inspiration over the centuries, the development of trade has been one of the foundations of the modern, globalized world in which we live. As the economic, social, and political importance of trade increased, so did the size, and geographic spread, of our organizations.

This growth, and the opportunities it provided, spawned a phenomenon called the multinational organization. These organizations, beginning with the East Indies Companies, both British and Dutch, which were created on the cusp of the 17th century, are capable of exercising extreme power not only in individual countries but globally. Countries, and often subnational regions, compete vigorously against one another for the establishment of facilities for a multinational organization for they bring increased revenue, employment, and economic activity.

These multinational organizations have established business operations in many different places for any one of a number of, or a combination of many, different reasons. These include, for example, taking advantage of new markets for their products or services, availing themselves of lower costs of production, being closer to sources of raw material, taking advantage of government incentives for business, reducing exposure to fluctuations in currency relationships, and lower taxes. The most pressing problem that these organizations face is that they have a national home where profits ultimately will have to come. In trying to bring the maximum amount of profit home, multinational organizations often engage in practices, particularly in relation to internal pricing, which frequently enrage either their host or home countries.

These internal pricing activities, known more commonly as transfer pricing, have provoked reactions from national jurisdictions to monitor and capriciously modify the internal-pricing activities of multinational organizations in ways that aim to protect their national income. This has often led to a discord that is so intense that at times it has caused managers to take their eye off the reason they are in business in the first place. Let's be clear, transfer pricing should not simply be about maximizing income. It is a much more important management issue than that, covering concerns such as management of competitive pressures, movement of funds between related organizations, repatriation of profits, and managing the effects of asymmetry in exchange rates in addition to reducing the impact of taxes and tariffs. Treated unwisely or with ignorance, transfer pricing is likely to lead to an incongruity in the added value of products and services as well as the crucial return on capital employed.

This book seeks to remind managers of these important issues and how easy it is to create friction between the interested parties if the pricing process is not properly thought out. I hope that you will indulge me in starting the book with a little look at history to understand how we arrived at where we are ... a time of increasing friction between the value creators and the regulators. It goes on to provide an insight into how such conflicts can be assuaged or avoided altogether by recognizing just how much international expansion adds to the complexity of doing business as a result of differences in culture, language, beliefs, regulatory frameworks, and requirements. Following this, it examines how changes in the business model will facilitate the development of transfer pricing as a strategic management tool and, by establishing a common language for the transfer pricing process, it may be used as one driver for creating added value throughout the organization.

Acknowledgments

For their indirect contribution, I am perpetually indebted to my students, past, present, and future, in both graduate and undergraduate classes, whose questions, comments, and witticisms contribute to the way I communicate the story I have to tell. They were, are, and always will be a source of inspiration to me.

I am also grateful to the team at Business Expert Press, particularly to David Parker, for unwavering faith in my ability and giving me the opportunity to produce this book; to Michael Czinkota whose encouraging early thoughts and ideas paved the way for what you will now read; to Professor Gary Knight for his insightful comments while this book was a work-in-process; and to Cindy Durand for her support, patience, and helpful advice during its creation.

Geoff Turner
Nicosia, Cyprus

CHAPTER 1

The International Organization

Introduction

As I indicated in the Preface to this book, I have chosen to start by looking into the past to try and understand why we have reached a point where transfer pricing is such a powerful, fractious issue in those organizations engaged in internal international trade. The conflicts this activity creates are both internal and external requiring a broad understanding of the underlying reasons if we are to manage them effectively. So I have chosen, over just a few pages, to look at history to better understand the environment that breeds these disputes. Please bear with me and enjoy the story.

Records show that business- and commerce-related activities were being carried out 3,000–6,000 years ago. Indeed, the Περίπλους τὴς Ἐρυθράς Θαλάσσης (The Periplus of the Erythraean Sea) is believed to have been written in the 1st century A.D., is a Greco-Roman document describing navigation and trading opportunities between cities along the coast of the Red Sea and Northeast Africa as well as across what we now know as the Indian Ocean to the west coast of India.

At the same time, the Arabian nomads, using camel trains, traversed Asia looking to trade their spices for Chinese silk opening up what was to become known as the Silk Road. For a long time, international trade was limited to the exchange of goods like textiles, food items, spices, precious metals, precious stones, and objects of art across both land and sea. Yet, the intention of this trade was not limited to generating economic value but satisfying political and social ambitions as well.

Just as society has developed through the centuries (see Figure 1.1), we have come a long way since those earlier times. Nevertheless, until the late 19th century, most of the world's working population was agricultural laborers who produced food and also knew how to fashion many

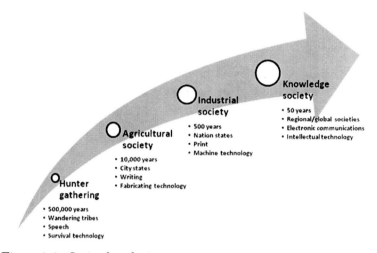

Figure 1.1. Societal evolution.

tools and other necessities. What they could not produce for themselves, they bought in neighboring towns in exchange for their agricultural surplus and a few handicrafts. Long-distance trading was rare because the output of all products was low and transportation was slow, expensive, and dangerous.

A little more than 100 years later, with the development of organizations, the evolution of technology, and the impact of globalization, international trade had taken on a remarkably new dimension. These events, all outside of any one country's control, have made it necessary for every country to engage in international trade for their economic and social survival. The journey from the *Land of Punt*[1] to the World Trade Organization (WTO) has been a long one and at each step along the way, people have responded to the changing times in their own inimitable way.

The Development of Trade

Pick up any item in a department store, whether it be a stuffed toy, a DVD player, or a fashion item, and check the *Made in* tag. The likelihood that it was manufactured in your country is slim. The chances are that the item was manufactured in China or assembled in Brazil. Even the food in your supermarket, whether fresh or prepackaged, may very well have been imported from another country.

We all know that international trade has been in vogue for centuries and most civilizations carried on trade with other parts of the world. This was necessary because the resources that communities needed either simply weren't available or could be obtained more competitively from other places. Rarely has any one community been entirely self-sufficient and in the present context, where technology and innovation in every aspect of business life have encouraged globalization, no country can afford to be isolated.

International trade has a rich history that started as a barter system, which was replaced by mercantilism in the 16th and 17th centuries. The 18th century saw a shift toward trade liberalism that, by and large, continued until the outbreak of the First World War. It was in this period that Adam Smith, the father of economics, wrote his famous book, *An Inquiry Into the Nature and Causes of the Wealth of Nations*. This book, published in 1776, did not especially focus on the benefits of developing trade itself but on the need to continuously improve the productive powers of a country, or an organization. This, he believed, would lead to an indefinite increase in the production of things to be consumed by individuals, which he saw as being good for any nation's economy. His vision came with a qualification however, which was that this would only be achieved in conjunction with a significant growth in local communities and the development of trade between them.

These thoughts were taken up about 40 years later by David Ricardo, perhaps the most influential economist of the time after Smith, who determined the relatively simple and coherent law of competitive advantage,[2] which suggests that total output will be increased if people and nations engage in those activities for which their advantages over others are the largest, or their disadvantages are the smallest. This principle remains valid in the 21st century and continues to influence international trade to the extent that the evolution of business activities in any country is more often than not shaped by a form of natural selection. Yet, the political process tends to bend the laws of nature as the government policies of each country seek to develop or protect industries or organizations through either export subsidies or import duties: practices that are gradually being eradicated as a result of the activities of the WTO.

Political posturing of this nature, although there was plenty of a different kind, was not especially evident throughout the long second half of the 19th century when most Western nations were actively promoting trade liberalization by reducing customs duties and abolishing quantitative restrictions. This allowed the trade of goods and services to go on freely and encouraged the establishment of business activities wherever it seemed best, both of which led to full employment and an improving quality of life. The result was the achievement of a level of international trade that many of the world's leading economies were not to experience again until the 1990s.[3]

Spectacular economic growth and the steady expansion of the global economy during this period led to an increase in the political aspirations of Empire. The resulting Great War changed the entire course of world trade as countries built walls around themselves with wartime controls. The effort put into dismantling wartime measures and getting international trade back to some sort of normality after the war was dramatically halted by the economic recession of 1920, which changed the balance of world trade once again. At this time, the rapid fluctuation in currency relationships, often resulting in devaluations, saw major changes in prosperity creating economic pressures that persuaded many countries to adopt protective mechanisms by raising, or reintroducing, duties, quotas, restrictions, and licensing, as well as introducing exchange controls to limit currency outflows.

The need to reverse this trend in protectionism and increase international trade between countries gave rise to the League of Nations–sponsored World Economic Conference in Geneva in May 1927. The attendees, from 29 nations, were neither delegates nor representatives of their respective countries but simply individuals who had gathered to determine what could be done to overcome the economic difficulties and conditions of the time. They engaged in a substantial dialogue that resulted in the development of a detailed and balanced multilateral trade agreement, which provided a prescription for the global economic ills they faced. Unfortunately, their work could only have practical consequences if it was translated into positive actions by their governments.

Regrettably, this agreement remained without practical effect due to the onset of the Great Depression in 1930. Throughout the ensuing decade, when economic activity initially fell dramatically (e.g., gross national product in the United States fell by 30% from 1930 to 1933), there was a global epidemic of protectionist measures. The planning of foreign trade, not just in communist societies but even in capitalist ones, came to be considered a normal function of the state. Mercantilist policies dominated the world scene until after the Second World War when trade agreements (the 1947 General Agreement on Tariffs and Trade) and supranational organizations (the 1957 Treaty of Rome that established the European Economic Community) became the chief means of managing and promoting international trade.

Today, the nature of international trade and the factors influencing global trade flows are much better understood. Global markets, which generally have their foundation in the natural resources that provide countries with a comparative competitive advantage, have been molded by many factors. These include the theories developed by economists— such as competitive advantage, and economies of scale—advances in technology both in terms of changes in product life cycles and methods of trade, as well as the structure of, and services provided by, the world's financial markets.

Think!

Does your organization regularly engage in international trade? Are you aware of all the factors that influence your global trade flows?

The Evolution of Organizations

Francois de la Rochefoucauld is attributed with the saying "The only constant in life, is change." Not only is this true of humans, it also applies to the evolution of organizations. In the Preface to this book, I declared that trade has been conducted in one form or another for all of recorded history. In all probability, it happened before then as well but one thing is certain, the development of trade has contributed to the modern, globalized world in which we live.

From the earliest times of business exchange, the trader, or peddler of goods, was known as a merchant. He, for he was almost universally a male, was a businessperson engaged in retail trade. The merchant would more often than not travel and traffic his wares between disparate communities. The Middle Ages saw the rapid expansion of trade as new land routes were opened by the Radhanites, the Frenchman Andrew of Longjumeau, the Flemish William of Rubruk as well as the Polo family from Italy, and many others. Later, expansion by sea was led by Vasco da Gama, Ferdinand Magellan, and, of course, Christopher Columbus. Although they may have been financed by others, all of them were, essentially, individual traders who became rich from trade. That the roads the merchants traveled were dangerous and full of pitfalls is an understatement and to combat this they formed the Merchant Guilds whose purpose was to negotiate for safe passage through the payment of regulated trade levies.

Later, these Guilds formed joint-stock companies, the earliest of which in the context of international trade were the East Indies Companies: both the British and the Dutch versions. Both companies were the enterprise of businessmen who joined forces to make money out of trade with South East Asia. From their formation on the cusp of the 17th century, these two companies grew to become imperial powers in their own right. Regrettably, abuse of market power, corporate greed, judicial impunity, and the destruction of traditional economies forced their national governments to rein them in toward the end of the 18th century. In both profound and disturbing ways, they provided the model for international trade and were the forerunners of the present day multinational enterprises (MNEs) even though they had one distinct advantage—they only paid taxes to one government—their one at home.

Present-day MNEs, which are those organizations that are based in one country (the home country) and have business operations in other countries (the host countries), continue to wield significant influence but it is perhaps a more insidious influence than that of their 17th-century counterparts. The current MNE has long been considered a threat to the egalitarianism of the free world simply because governments compete to win their investment. These commercial organizations have so much influence in generating jobs and revenues that a range of social issues such as accounting practices, labor relations, taxation policies, development plans, and community infrastructure are determined by their concerns. They are rarely concerned with the interplay of supply and demand but are simply looking for ways to maximize returns to owners, more of which later, by squeezing the sources of supply.

As we stagger through the early years of the 21st century, in commercial situations other than where the investment required is significant, individuals, entrepreneurs, and big companies are mixing and matching together all sorts of technologies, markets, and innovations to start new businesses out of nowhere or give old businesses some totally new dimension. This trend is becoming one of the most powerful drivers of the global economy, nurturing more small- and medium-sized enterprises with a global reach than anyone realizes. How does this happen? Rather simply actually for, with a modest amount of capital, the right imagination, and sufficient Internet bandwidth, anyone can assemble a global commercial enterprise by matching providers and customers from anywhere to do anything for anyone.[4] Conceivably, we have come a full circle, returning to the world of the individual merchant. The key difference is the technology available to conduct trade, which these days just happens to be so much more than peddling goods.

If this really is the case, the notion of transfer pricing may have become irrelevant for it is a business concept that typically only applies to organizations, either singular or in a group, with a presence in more than one location, whether they are in the same country or in different nations, and where there are business transactions between those locations. That would seem to rule out the relevance of this book to many but please keep reading anyway because there are still an awful lot of huge organizations for whom the discussion is useful as well as many situations in smaller enterprises where application of the principles I'll discuss later may lead to a better understanding of their value chain.

Think!

If you work in a smaller enterprise where there is only one operational location, can you think of situations, particularly related to performance measurement, when the use of transfer pricing principles might come in handy?

In Search of Increasing Profits

The demand for commercial organizations to produce ever-increasing profits has become incessant. If you don't believe that, then open your Internet search engine and put in the words *the need for increased profitability*. Using Google, the return was more than 96 million results in a fraction more than one-tenth of a second. Yahoo! provided an even greater return of 187 million results and many, if not most of them, were promoting ways to increase profits. Our capitalist system has a lot to answer for!

Francis Fukuyama[5] has a view on that and he is convinced that the triumph of the West, Western ideas, and the alleged exhaustion of viable alternatives to liberalism has anointed capitalism as the dominant social, economic, and political system of this era. Remember, the main rule in capitalism is to increase profits as quickly as possible and the driving forces behind capitalism are our commercial organizations. Those most prominent are the multinational and transnational corporations listed on various bourses around the world, which, goaded by financial markets, are obsessed with the creation of ever greater annual profit. Figure 1.2 provides a simple illustration of this obsession, which is achieved through the creation of a variety of networks, the optimization of advances in information technologies, and, quite often with the support of national governments, the exploitation of poorer communities and the destruction of trade barriers.

Recognizing the fact that they are essentially private organizations, governments have created laws to require these organizations to prioritize the welfare of their owners above all else. In commercial parlance, this translates to increasing their wealth, in itself usually accomplished

Figure 1.2. Demanding more and more.

by growing the profitability of the organization. This has become a systemic requirement of capitalism that is being achieved through the use of a variety of strategies, such as financial engineering; cost reduction; and even tax minimization, avoidance, and evasion. The commercial organization has become very powerful indeed, perhaps even more powerful today than the East Indies Companies were at their pinnacle.

Yet, the power of these organizations is not necessarily being used in the wider social interest. Although created through law and numerous social contracts, these organizations do not owe allegiance to any nation, community, or locality, yet they clearly recognize the increased dependence of their host on private capital to stimulate economic activity. It seems that all the best cards are in the hands of commercial organizations and they utilize them to the fullest to extract the greatest profit possible. Despite the claimed advances in transparency, accountability, and corporate social responsibility, bending the rules to enhance the wealth of owners is not unheard of and in many quarters is seen as an entrepreneurial skill. Nowhere is this more evident than in the establishment of transfer prices in MNEs.

Changes in the Transfer Pricing Model

In the years leading to the end of the 20th century, transfer pricing was almost always associated with the exchange of goods between different divisions or subsidiaries of the same organization. The base for determining an acceptable transfer price was the sum of direct costs and variable overhead (or full costs in some cases) with a margin or a markup added to cover other costs and give some profit to the originating division or subsidiary. There was rarely any consistency in application. Transfer prices from the supply units, such as component factories or production units, to assembly or sales units were calculated differently depending on whether it related to deliveries to a new unit or delivery of a new product to a unit where there was already an established relationship. Depending on the maturity and profit situation of the receiving units, transfer prices were set up differently.

Quite possibly, there were good business reasons for such variability. As long as they were well understood within the organization's management circles and performance-measurement criteria reflected the differences, it didn't present much of a problem. With the passing of time, the structure of organizations, whether local, regional, national, multinational, or transnational, and the nature of their operations changed. These changes resulted in a streamlining of business processes, usually by way of simplification and standardization. Organizational doctrine insisted on a focus on core activities, which led to an increase in outsourcing and subcontracting, particularly between units of the same parent organization. The outcome, quite naturally, was an increased focus on transfer pricing principles and their meaning.

Furthermore, with the spread of globalization, the exchange of goods between different units of the same organization intensified, raising the issue of transfer pricing even higher on the management team's agenda. From the discussions and debates on this developing business problem came an opinion which suggested that transfer prices should be equal for all receiving entities. But why? The circumstances surrounding each and every situation requiring a transfer price, as it is with assorted external customers, was likely to be different. How could an identical transfer price be acceptable in all cases?

Unfortunately, the vagaries of transfer pricing were becoming a topic of interest in places other than inside commercial organizations. Revenue authorities in the supplying or receiving country, or both, were becoming increasingly concerned with transfer pricing being used as a vehicle for manipulating profits resulting in reduced tax revenues. This was particularly noticeable when there were significant differences in the marginal tax rates of the countries involved. The cost factor attributable to government, represented by taxation, in all of its guises, now became a significant factor in determining transfer prices.

No matter what was being transferred from one unit to another across jurisdictional boundaries, revenue authorities were asking pointed questions about the transfer price—what was the underlying cost of the item being transferred and what was the margin or markup and how was it determined? Initially lacking clear rules or understanding, these investigations placed organizations under increasing pressure to justify transfer prices and led to an increasing number of disputes with the revenue authorities because the old principles were no longer always valid. Looking to reduce the frequency and cost of these disputes, many revenue authorities, especially those with substantial resources, sought to establish rules and guidelines for the taxation of cross-border transactions between related organizations in an MNE.

Think!

Does your organization actively engage in cross-border transfer pricing? How much of the time taken to determine the relevant transfer price is devoted to taxation concerns?

An internationally accepted approach to the problem by revenue authorities was to insist that organizations price related party international dealings in the same way that truly independent parties would have done in the same situation: in other words, using the arm's length principle. In this way, it was thought that pricing for international dealings between related parties would reflect a fair return for the activities carried out, the assets used, and the risks assumed in carrying out these activities.

Unfortunately, the outcome in many instances was artificial transfer prices determined to satisfy the revenue authorities. This resulted in the distortion of organizational performance leading to imperfect or unreasonable business decisions. One area in particular, that of research and development, suffered from these transfer pricing policies. They led to an imbalance among investment, costs, and profit because of a failure to reflect the impact of intellectual capital and how it added value to products and services. The only way this is likely to be rectified is through the development of a suitable frame of reference for value-related transfer pricing while at the same time eliminating many of the elements of risk.

Harmony or Conflict?

In a global economy where MNEs play a prominent role, governments are keen to ensure that the taxable profits of these organizations are not artificially shifted out of their jurisdiction. The revenue authorities also need to be satisfied that the reported tax base in their country reflects the economic activity undertaken by the local unit(s) of the MNE. In 2004, Australia, Canada, the United Kingdom, and the United States of America formed the Washington-based Joint International Tax Shelter Information Centre (JITSIC) in a bid to stem the flow of cross-border revenue losses. The objective of JITSIC is to deter promotion of, and investment in, abusive tax schemes through information exchange and knowledge sharing.

Driven by the impact of the current financial crisis, cash-strapped governments around the world are aggressively targeting transfer pricing in their jurisdictions. In early 2010, the Obama administration announced that it was stepping up the Inland Revenue Service's review activities in an attempt to recover US$12 billion of the estimated US$60 billion in tax that is avoided through transfer pricing every year. Canada also has cracked down on MNEs that dodge tax through inflating profits or losses in dealings with their related companies overseas by imposing the full tax rate, plus a penalty. The Australian Taxation Office sees a risk that MNEs will shift Australian profits to subsidiaries that suffered losses in the global financial crisis and has been conducting transfer pricing audits to protect their revenue base.

Think!
If you practice substantial cross-border transfer pricing, have you faced problems like this? What impact did it have on your organization?

Despite revenue authorities' determination to wage war on transfer pricing around the world, it is significant that they have lost the last couple of battles[6] when MNEs have decided to fight back in the courts. For these organizations, it is essential to limit the risks of double taxation that may result from a dispute between two countries on the determination of the arm's-length remuneration for their cross-border transactions with associated enterprises. Recognizing this, the Organisation for Economic Co-operation and Development (OECD) released transfer pricing guidelines[7] that elaborate on the arm's-length principle and provide methodologies to evaluate an arm's-length transfer price.

However, in reality, the application and interpretation of the arm's-length standard varies among OECD member countries with a number of them setting up more detailed transfer pricing regulations. One thing is sure, transfer pricing is highly subject to interpretation and judgment making it hard, if not impossible, to find the *right* answer. This absence of uniform practices among tax administrations has caused transfer pricing issues to become a real bone of contention between MNEs and revenue authorities. What is more, these variations in practice have become a prime area for international conflict between the revenue authorities themselves.

These conflicts of interest will continue to give rise to many disputes between MNEs and the revenue authorities that will inevitably find their way into the courts in search of settlement. Ultimately, every MNE needs to make a decision about its approach to the thorny issue of transfer pricing. This is likely to be influenced by the organization's size, the extent of its foreign related party dealings, its attitude to risk, and the desired relationship with the revenue authorities in each jurisdiction in which it operates. The outcome will surely have an impact on its structure and strategy as the organization seeks to mitigate the regulatory risk of cross-border transactions.

Summary

We have seen many changes in the nature of organizations over time and there can be little doubt that we shall see many more in the years to come. Changes in technology, the physical environment, and the regulatory environment will ensure that this happens. Come what may, there will always be conflict between commercial organizations, of whatever size, and the revenue authorities over matters pertaining to taxation. The key issue relates to the extent of those disagreements and whether they can be resolved amicably or by judicial means.

Perhaps, one of the most important factors in determining that key issue is the regulatory style of the revenue authorities. The continuum of that style is bounded at one end by a close consultative relationship and by adversarial legalism at the other. Neither is particularly satisfactory and so the starting point should probably be where all parties see the law as an instrument of legitimate policy to be respected. This does not presuppose that one side or the other is the protagonist in this conflict but that both need a change in attitude if there is to be any chance of harmony.

To achieve this, it first requires changes in revenue authorities' attitudes toward taking a more cooperative approach to MNEs, which may help them change their attitude toward the revenue authorities. They may then regard the revenue authorities as legitimate agents of the law rather than as players of perpetual tax games and so refrain from considering tax legislation as material to work on. This may lead to greater transparency and accountability between both parties from which it becomes possible to build a trusting relationship that forms an essential part of an MNE's transfer pricing management policies.

Such a change is unlikely to eventuate unless there is some form of supranational regulatory framework to create more uniformity in transfer pricing regulation across diverse regulatory cultures. Mutual cooperation and coordination between revenue authorities in international tax enforcement is being seen as increasingly essential in the context of overcoming the difficulties that MNEs face in complying with the law. It should lead to a significant reduction in the compliance burden, uncertainty surrounding transfer pricing issues, and penalty risks. Failure to progress such a change is likely to result in a rethink of organizational structure and a resurgence in the use of low-tax jurisdictions by those organizations for which significant structural change is improbable.

CHAPTER 2

The Theory of Transfer Pricing

Introduction

Around the world, the things we buy increasingly have a transnational source. People in Japan wear Levi's, while Americans drive Toyotas and Cypriots eat Dutch fruit. Yet, despite the fact that we are consuming more international products than ever before, one of the ways in which nations remain distinct is in how high or low prices are in their local markets. That Chilean wine costs more in Nicosia than Santiago should come as no surprise. It has longer to travel and more associated costs in getting it to market. The same applies to other important consumer goods, such as petrol and flour, yet local products are not always the cheapest. We like to think that the closer a product is to its source, the less it will cost but that rationale does not apply all the time. Let's look at Apple's iPod Nano. It is made in China or Taiwan for US and British markets. The costs associated with bringing it to market in either country are relatively similar. So why does one cost so much more in Britain than the United States?[1]

Much of the difference is related to tariffs and consumption taxes, or the lack thereof, which affect the price. But it is not just these. Another reason is currency valuation. Right now, the US dollar is weak compared with many other currencies; so, in theory, items bought there should cost more, yet, as we have seen with the iPod Nano example, that is not always so. In the case of most consumer goods, the price at which they are sold generally reflects the varying levels of consumer purchasing power in individual countries. If this were true, the iPod Nano, while more expensive in some countries, ought to have a comparable cost in terms of actual purchasing power. Logically then, we would expect prices to be lower across the board in poorer countries and more expensive in wealthier nations. However, this is not always the case as we can see from Figure 2.1 where the iPod Nano prices in some selected countries, both rich and poor, are shown.

Another factor that needs to be considered is the MNEs' pricing strategy. In this, organizations have a lot of discretion when it comes to setting prices. There is nothing to stop them setting dramatically different prices in different places in order to make the most profit. In other words, an organization will charge more for a product in one market than another because it knows consumers have no alternative. What is more, retailers selling the organization's products can also charge more if they feel that consumers will bear the cost.

Such is the cutthroat world of commercial trade, where an organization's ability to establish an acceptable pricing policy for its products, services, or both is a crucial element of business sustainability. Many worry that they are asking too much and yet underpricing hurts as much as overpricing does. If the price of your product or service is too high, potential customers will look for a more affordable alternative. On the other hand, if the price is too low, potential customers will think it cannot be that good. Here I am reminded of the story of *Goldilocks and the Three Bears*, where, on entering the house of the three bears in search of food,

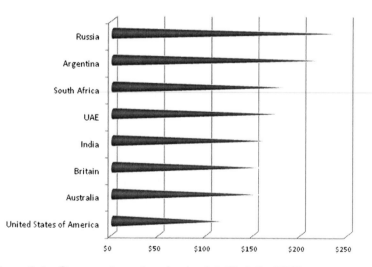

Figure 2.1. Comparative prices for Apple's iPod (in US$).

Goldilocks sees three bowls of porridge on the table. On trying the first bowl, she declares it too hot. The porridge in the second bowl is too cold for her but in the third bowl, it is "just right." Pricing is exactly like that. It may be too high, it may be too low, or it may be just right. And, just as Goldilocks decided on the choice of porridge bowl, the buyer of an organization's products, services, or both will decide on the rightness of the price.

It has always been this way. If an organization operates under conditions of perfect competition, it has no choice but to accept the price a buyer is prepared to offer. At the other extreme, if an organization is a monopolist, then it can set any price it chooses. The reality is usually somewhere in between and, as such, the asking price needs to be very carefully considered relative to those of close competitors. Of course, that is not all an organization has to think about. The asking price must also take into consideration the total cost of providing that product or service—something that is rarely known but is often guessed.

They are just two of the aspects of pricing. A third relates to the investment necessary to deliver your products or services to the customer and the return required on that investment. This is only one more complexity in an already intricate environment. Nonetheless, to price your products, services, or both appropriately, you must understand how much your customer is willing to pay, what it costs you to provide, what investment is involved, and the return required by the financiers of that investment. So let us consider each of these pricing fundamentals, and how they interact, in a little more detail.

Think!
Do you really know the full cost of your products or services? Do your selling prices absolutely depend on knowing this?

Understanding Your Customers' Needs

Let's be clear about one thing right now: It is not just the asking price that a buyer considers when deciding whether to purchase a product or service. It is that and everything else, such as quality, exactness of fit, and delivery time, which goes along with the product or service being bought. It is easy to make assumptions about what customers want and need but that is not the way to go. You need to understand customer priorities, and clarify their likes and dislikes if you are to secure the best possible price from your customer. Knowing what they are, for each of your customers, is important because their purchasing function is one vital link in their organization's value chain. As such, the buyer must understand if the total cost of using your product or service allows them to add value for their organization in a meaningful way.

Think!

Do you really know your customers? Do you have a system that records their buying needs? Do your selling prices take these needs into consideration?

Of course, not only will your product or service have a different impact on each customer's value chain but also each of your customers will have different expectations of how their needs should be met. What is more, the impact of your product or service and their needs will change over time and so your pricing must also change along with them even if there are no changes in the other aspects of price determination.

Knowing the Cost of Things

It is probably best to start this section by asking *what is meant by cost?* The answer to this question may seem, at first sight, very obvious. Most readers will say that cost is how much was paid for an item of goods being supplied or a service being provided. Unfortunately, it is not that simple. In the context of our organization, cost may be explained as the valuation in money terms of the effort, material, use of long-lived resources, consumption of utilities, wasted time, risks incurred, and opportunities foregone in making a product or service available to our customers.

For all organizations, one of the key essentials in determining our selling prices is to know the total cost of each of our products or services. This total cost is made up of two distinct components: There are those costs that are driven by a particular cost object and those costs that maintain our support functions. Let's pause for a moment because I've used some terminology that you may not be familiar with. What do I mean by *cost object*? Many of you will immediately associate this term with the products or services your organization sells. That would be a reasonable starting point. On the other hand, they may not be the prime drivers of the money that you spend. I'm sure that in a number of organizations, especially service organizations, it is your customers, and their requirements, that really drive your cash out-flows. If this is the case, then the customer is your cost object.

Think!
What is the primary cost object in your firm? Is it possible for us to have multiple cost objects? How might we try to manage that?

Nevertheless, whatever our cost object, we need to break down our total cost into those costs that are readily traceable to our cost object—the *direct costs*—and those costs that are necessary to support our productive activities but that we are not able to readily trace to our cost object—the *indirect costs*, which are often referred to as *overheads*. Figure 2.2 provides a graphical illustration of where the particular costs of a professional services organization, such as a law firm, might lie. In this case, the cost object is the customer, whereas in a manufacturing firm, the cost objects are more likely to be the products that are made. Any item of cost may be either direct or indirect depending on its traceability to a particular cost object. As a result of their traceability, direct costs are usually considered to be *variable costs* because they increase or decrease in line with changes in the level of activity of the cost object.

Indirect costs, on the other hand, are more likely to remain unchanged in the face of moderately changing levels of activity and so are considered *fixed costs*. Since it is imperative, in the longer term, that we recover all of our costs to remain profitable, it is important that we have an appropriate mechanism to allocate these indirect, or fixed, costs to our cost objects in order to understand the full cost. This process of allocation is a significant problem for many organizations because it is not easy to understand how much of their indirect costs are consumed by their cost objects. If it was understandable, then we would probably consider them direct costs and our problem would go away.

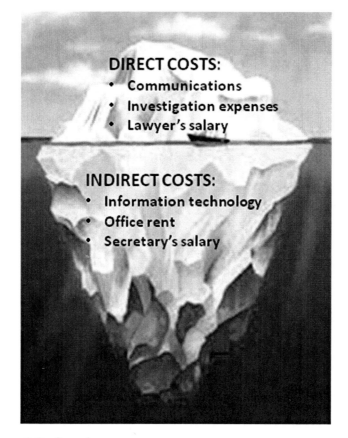

Figure 2.2. Cost elements.

Unfortunately, when using the total cost concept as a determinant of selling prices, this arbitrary allocation of indirect costs often results in misleading information about the total cost of a cost object. This, in turn, leads to inappropriate prices being offered for our goods or services. Indeed, on this basis, some folks like to say: *Well, we'd have these costs anyway. Why should we include them in the cost of our products and services?* The answer is simple: Indirect costs add up and significantly affect profitability. What is more, some products or services we sell consume significantly more overhead than others, which makes the perceived profitability of those products often inaccurate.

To make it easier for us to establish selling prices, we should strive to identify as many costs as possible in the direct category but, since we do need to understand the total cost of the things we sell, we may still be left with the need to allocate some costs. How should we go about that? Traditionally, the most common methods of allocating indirect cost have been based on a relevant direct input such as labor hours, or machine hours, or units of material. Old traditions die hard but the nature of our competitive environment is changing rapidly and the ways of old are proving insufficiently flexible to deal with the complexity encountered in our modern organizations.

Think!
How does your organization allocate indirect costs? Is that method really suitable for your business environment?

There are a variety of costing systems available for us to use,[2] one or more of which will be relevant for our organizational situation. What is absolutely clear is that if we do not properly understand the cost of making a product or service available to our customers, we are likely to develop inappropriate pricing and marketing strategies. Even so, it is not essential to have the most accurate cost system. The aim should be to consistently understand the cost of making a product or service available to our customers, accurate to within 5% or 10%. The idea is to have the most effective costing system, one that balances the cost of errors made from inaccurate measurements with the cost of measurement. Getting close to understanding our true costs is exceedingly more valuable than not including any part of that cost in our pricing calculations.

Risk and Return

Taking risks is a necessary part of conducting business, with the level of return being the compensation for the degree of risk being taken. The specter of constant change or the acceptance that risks are a part of our everyday organizational life should not be taken as a reason for doing nothing about risk. At the very least, we need to identify every risk that our organization is exposed to whether they are market risks or exchangeable risks.

In the context of pricing goods and services, risk expresses itself in the variability, or potential variability, in the products or services we supply and the customers we supply to. Put more simply, our products may become unfashionable or too expensive, and our customers may change their business strategy or close up shop altogether leaving us with products that we can't sell or debts that we can't collect. When these circumstances change, a different set of risks is created, which may be either greater or less than the risk that has been eliminated. Our pricing activity needs to consider these possibilities when deciding on the return required at either a product or a customer level. Where the perceived degree of risk, whether it be product or customer related, is higher, selling prices need to command a premium over the prices charged for those products or services, or to those customers, seen to be less of a risk.

Think!

Do you take differential risk into account when determining prices in your organization? How do you do it?

Furthermore, when considering the returns required from a particular selling activity, an additional aspect to consider is the extent of your investment in both the product or service and the customer. This will usually comprise investment in long-lived resources, whether for the organization as a whole or specifically for a product, service, or customer, as well as supplies, work-in-process, and monies due from the customer. The funding for this investment comes from our investors, either in the form of equity or debt, who require compensation for investing their funds with us. For every organization, the extent of this compensation reflects the average of the cost of debt and the cost of equity weighted in their market-value proportions. As such, it represents the rate of return we must earn on the resources employed in our organization to meet the expectations of our investors.

There is little doubt that the level of investment varies between products and services as well as between customers and so the prices we charge should reflect the financing cost of the relevant level of investment. In so doing, if the prices we establish are too high, then we need to look for ways to reduce the investment for we cannot accept lower returns. To do so would not allow us to compensate our investors appropriately, which may probably lead them to withdraw their funding with the potential to ultimately force us out of business.

Moving from External to Internal Pricing

Unreasonably, when it comes to internal pricing, many organizations continue to approach their pricing decisions in terms of *adding something on to the cost*. Cost in this context is almost always the total cost, which in many cases is an imprecise and significantly inaccurate value on which to base a selling-price decision. In reality, setting selling prices is concerned with establishing the best price that a prospective end customer will pay for our product or service as well as knowing the lowest price that is acceptable.

By comparing the selling price we think may be achieved with our cost estimate, we are in a position to understand whether making the sale is likely to give us the return we require on our investment in the business. Where we lack accurate or complete market price information for our product or service, our own costs will be helpful in determining a selling price as long as we believe that these costs are typical and competitive. In practice, most organizations approach the determination of selling prices through a combination of market research and costing.

On occasions, the market selling price will be lower than the projected selling price derived from the cost of our product or service plus the margin necessary to provide for an adequate return on our investment. In these situations, we shall need to decide whether to:

- accept a lower price, margin, and return on investment;
- explore ways of reducing our costs;
- explore ways to differentiate our product or service, which is in effect changing our market positioning.

If we decide to explore ways of reducing our costs, we need to look for ways of increasing efficiency in purchasing, production, or distribution. On the other hand, if we are happy that our cost information reflects reality and that our operational processes are highly efficient, then we have to accept that our competitors, who are selling at lower prices, are willing to accept a lower margin and probably a lower return on their investment. In this situation, we need to reflect on our strategy and position in the market.

I have tried to make it clear that price decisions, both internal and external, are a combination of market research, competitive analysis, and cost information. In determining selling prices, we are attempting to achieve our strategic objectives and return on investment through maximizing our market share, taking into consideration such factors as our own resources and capabilities, competitive prices, market demand, strategies available, as well as social and legal issues. We supplement these factors by continually monitoring our sales volume, sales mix, and actual performance and feeding the information collected back into our pricing model. Setting the right price for our products or services is undoubtedly one of the most challenging activities in any organization and even more so when we are required to consider two or more related organizations involved in the delivery of the final product to our end customer.

It is essential to set prices that will simultaneously make us competitive within our own market and allow us to grow revenue. Achieving this delicate balance means knowing not only our costs, but also the state of our industry and the overall economy. Most importantly, it means knowing our industry and our business in considerable depth, as well as our end customers and what it takes to convince them to buy.

All of these factors underlie the organizational and behavioral issues that need to be taken into consideration in any discussion that takes place inside an organization in relation to transfer pricing. To meet their organization's overall objective of maximizing shareholder wealth, managers need to be ever vigilant for ways of improving efficiency and effectiveness, and hence profitability, usually through cost reduction or business change programs. There is no question that in multiproduct, multi-process organizations, a divisionalized structure, where each division is of a much more manageable size and is regarded as a profit center, is more advantageous in these circumstances.

Nevertheless, it is inevitable that all divisions are not totally independent and this creates particular difficulties in measuring divisional performance and in avoiding actions by divisional managers that are detrimental to the organization as a whole. The alternative, which requires some degree of interference in divisional management's affairs, inevitably waters down the benefits of this form of organizational structure and undermines managerial independence. Yet, to be fair, each of the divisions in such a structure cannot be totally independent for it is part of the organization as a whole.

Compromise between divisional independence and corporate coordination is absolutely essential to prevent suboptimal behavior by divisional managers who often circumvent the organizational ethos in search of better results for their division, and greater rewards for themselves, to the detriment of overall organizational performance. Nowhere is this more evident than in the thorny issue of transfer pricing, which has implications for the organization as a whole at all levels from strategic planning through to supply chain management.

The Reason for Transfer Pricing

Transfer pricing exists because of the interdependence I talked about before. This impacts many organizations, not just the multinationals, because it creates a problem in determining at what price goods and services are transferred between divisions. The reason for transfer pricing is to meet several needs of the organization as a whole.

Think!

Are you wondering what the rewards are for going through the stress of getting the right transfer price for goods and services that move around your organization?

The primary objective of transfer pricing is to ensure that, while respecting and protecting the autonomy of the divisions, we are able to redistribute the economic resources within the organization in such a way that we are able to maximize the wealth of our owners. Of course, this will only ever be achieved by making sure that our divisional managers are motivated into making good economic decisions themselves. What do I mean by *good* in this context? Well, obviously, divisional managers need to make decisions that improve the profit of their own division but good decisions are those that also ensure an improvement in the financial performance of the organization as a whole. This idea of good decisions stretches to concerns over matters such as management of competitive pressures, movement of funds between related organizations, repatriation of profits, and managing the effects of asymmetry in exchange rates in addition to reducing the impact of taxes and tariffs.

MNEs are in a position to utilize their presence in different countries, especially low-cost ones, to lower input costs through structured transfer pricing so that they can match or undercut local competition in the supply of the finished product. In order to improve their overall competitiveness, MNEs often utilize extremely low transfer prices not only to create, in certain markets, a price advantage but also to improve their business reputation and increase their market competitiveness in the receiving country. This is generally a market-entry strategy in order to take business from competitors and to expand the international status of the MNE.

For political or other reasons, such as avoiding the distribution of excessive profits to local shareholders, MNEs may prefer to invest funds in one country rather than another. Transfer pricing, usually by way of artificially higher input prices or artificially lower selling prices, provides an indirect way of shifting funds into, or out of, a particular country. Not wishing to accumulate too much profit in an international subsidiary is not just about sharing these profits with local shareholders, it may also present problems when trying to bring those profits back to home base for distribution to the organization's owners.

Many smaller, developing countries have capital controls in place to limit the flow of foreign capital into, and more importantly, out of their country. For this reason, MNEs use transfer pricing as a mechanism for limiting profits earned by their international operations in countries where such controls exist. While trying to achieve these specific objectives, disputes are likely to arise between the MNEs and the revenue authorities in the relevant countries resulting in a reduction in overall organizational effectiveness and profitability. Something to avoid at all times!

For MNEs, one of their biggest risk exposures is the exchange, and holding of numerous foreign currencies. In recent years, global foreign exchange markets have exhibited considerable volatility, and with currency relationships between various countries fluctuating very largely and frequently, MNEs are exposed to an unacceptably large foreign exchange risk. This risk is not only related to trade transactions but also in the translation of foreign currency–based asset and liability values. Through the timing of their payments, MNEs have the opportunity to select an appropriate exchange rate to pay and transfer pricing enhances the effectiveness of this approach, enabling MNEs to further reduce their risk. Through astute management, MNEs are able to structure transfer pricing arrangements in such a way as to mitigate their exposure to fluctuating foreign exchange relationships. This is not such a bad thing but the management of foreign exchange exposures for an MNE is a relatively complex centralized function, the costs of which need to be considered in any transfer pricing model.

Perhaps, the most common use of transfer pricing, and probably the foundation of many an MNEs' transfer pricing policies, is to reduce their overall tax liability. The objective is to maximize profits in countries where the tax burden is lower, thus reducing the tax expense of the organization as a whole. Yet, there is another side to this coin where product transfers are concerned and that is the tariffs that will be payable on the imported goods, which sometimes are considerable. As I mentioned earlier in the book, this interplay provides fertile ground for conflict, which creates a serious side issue that takes the organization's managers' eyes off the main game—that of maximizing the return to the owners of the enterprise.

Think!

How many of these reasons form the basis of determining the transfer pricing policy in your organization?

In this regard, effective transfer pricing will be a more powerful tool than ever before, in large part precisely because of the economy or perhaps more accurately, the financial crisis and the associated credit crunch. Across the world, banks have sharply curtailed lending, even to well-established commercial organizations. As a result, credit is hard to come by and cash is king. In these situations, every organization, whatever its size, needs to recognize that making the most prudent use of its available cash-management tools is critical and transfer pricing is one of those.

Transfer pricing policies play a vital role in determining the overall profitability, and associated cash flow, of an MNE. One transfer pricing policy may result in a large amount of income and cash remaining with a particular division. On the other hand, a different policy may result in a more beneficial allocation of income and surplus cash being returned to the parent company where it may be put to more effective use. The distribution of an organization's income and cash that makes sense when the economy is booming and credit is plentiful may no longer make sense in a slow growth environment with tight credit markets.

Effective transfer pricing policies should be structured around the underlying economics of an organization's business model. Over time, due to changes in the business model, as well as external economic and financial conditions, those underlying economics will be different and transfer pricing policies need to be modified to reflect that. Given the dramatic changes in the economic environment since 2009, transfer pricing policies should have already been reviewed to better align with changed economic realities and organizational objectives.

Think!

There has been a global upheaval in recent times that will almost certainly have changed business models. Has yours changed? If so, how have you realigned your transfer pricing policy?

Of course, changes to economic reality do not just affect commercial organizations. Around the world, national governments are feeling the pinch too! It's no secret that tax revenues are generally in a state of decline and revenue authority employees are being exhorted to chase every possible source of revenue. Particularly juicy targets are those organizations they consider to be foreign, such as local operations of an MNE or even the foreign parent itself. After all, if you can raise money for your own jurisdiction by taking it from organizations or tax authorities that live far away, the local political consequences of a step-up in tax-collection activity are likely to be more favorable. So we should expect revenue authorities around the world to be increasingly aggressive in examining the transfer pricing policies of organizations in their jurisdictions. Enforcement pressures around the world will continue to rise sharply.[3]

Internally, of course, we need to provide useful, transparent, and well-documented information that will not only aid the evaluation of managerial and economic performance of our divisions but also assist in risk mitigation and optimization of organizational cash management. Externally, we need to show that our transfer pricing policies do not prejudice the revenue authorities in one jurisdiction over those in another. This is why there is no better time than the present for organizations to think very carefully about transfer pricing. Get it right and it can be a highly successful way of supporting cost reduction or business change programs—get it wrong and it may prove to be a very expensive mistake both internally, in terms of management motivation, and externally in the form of compliance costs and penalties imposed by revenue authorities.

Transfer Pricing Options

Our transfer pricing policy needs to eliminate the possibility of any ambiguity, particularly when it comes to specifying the sourcing rules for the various divisions that make up the organization's family. At one end of the spectrum, an organization may mandate internal transactions and at the other end, it will allow divisions' discretion whether to buy or sell externally. The policy also needs to define the rules for calculating a transfer price. There are three general methods available although it is also possible for an alternative method to be applied in different circumstances.

Market-based transfer pricing, or an arm's-length price, is the preferred method of revenue authorities around the world and is most commonly used when the outside market for the product or service is well defined, competitive, and stable. Yet, it is not unusual for organizations to only use the market price as an upper boundary for the transfer price. Market-based transfer prices normally align divisional managers' incentives with need to maximize overall organizational profit and are more commonly accepted when divisions have discretion in their purchasing arrangements.

The selling division is generally indifferent between receiving the market price from an external customer and receiving the same price from an internal customer. As such, the deciding factor is whether the buying division is willing to pay the market price. If they are unwilling to pay the market price, the implication is that organizational profit is maximized when the selling division sells the product in the external market, even if this leaves the buying division idle.

In most cases, there are cost savings on internal transfers compared with external sales. These savings usually arise because the selling division can avoid such expenses as a customer credit check and collection efforts, and the buying division might avoid incurring inspection costs in the receiving department. Market-based transfer pricing continues to align managerial incentives with organizational goals even in the presence of these cost savings if appropriate adjustments are made to the market-based transfer price to reflect these cost savings.

Of course, there will be circumstances when it is not possible to use this method because market prices are not readily available. This is frequently the case with the internal sale of intermediate products and many services. In these circumstances, one of the alternative pricing mechanisms has to be used.

Negotiated transfer pricing has the advantage of emulating a free market in which divisional managers buy and sell from each other in a manner that simulates arm's-length transactions. However, there is no reason to assume that the outcome of these transfer price negotiations will serve the best interests of the organization as a whole. The transfer price may very well depend on which divisional manager is the better poker player rather than whether the transfer results in profit-maximizing production and sourcing decisions. With this possibility in mind, many organizations prefer to mediate the negotiation process and, should divisional managers fail to reach an agreement on price even though the transfer is in the best interests of the organization, impose a transfer price.

Cost-based transfer pricing can also align managerial incentives with organizational goals as long as various factors are properly considered, including the external-market opportunities for both divisions and possible capacity constraints of the selling division. In the absence of an established market price, many organizations base the transfer price on the output cost of the selling division. Of course, this simply begs the question of *what do we mean by cost?* This is an issue that we shall come back to later in the book but for now I'll explain the ideas behind cost-based transfer pricing by looking at a couple of potential situations.

Think!

Before we do, which option does your company use for its transfer pricing? Does it create disputes between divisions? If you use cost-based transfer pricing, what do you mean by cost?

First, consider the case in which the selling division sells an intermediate product to external customers as well as to the buying division. In this situation, an understanding of capacity constraints is crucial. If the selling division has excess capacity, a cost-based transfer price using the variable cost of supply will align incentives because it will be indifferent about the transfer, and the buying division will fully incorporate the organization's incremental cost of making the intermediate product in its production and marketing decisions. Of course, if the selling division has a capacity constraint, transfers to the buying division will displace external sales. In this case, in order to align incentives, the opportunity cost of these lost sales must be passed on to the buying division, which is accomplished by setting the transfer price equal to the selling division's external-market sales price.

Second, consider the case in which there is no external market for the selling division. If it is to be treated as a profit center, it must be allowed the opportunity to recover its full cost of production plus a reasonable profit. If the buying division is charged the full cost of production, incentives are aligned unless it can either source the intermediate product for a lower cost elsewhere, or it cannot generate a reasonable profit on the sale of the final product when it pays the selling division's full cost of production for the intermediate product.

Let's look more deeply into this second situation. Where the buying division can source the intermediate product for a lower cost elsewhere, and the selling division's full cost of production reflects its future long-run average cost, the company should consider closing down the selling division. Alternatively, if the problem lies in the ability of the buying division to generate an acceptable profit, after including the selling division's full cost of production for the intermediate product in its total cost, on the sale of the final product, the optimal organizational decision might be to close the selling division and stop production and sale of the final product. However, if either the selling division or the buying division manufactures and markets multiple products, the analysis becomes more complex and may quite often result in internal disputes that lead to a failure to consummate a deal to the overall detriment of the organization. There has to be a way of resolving these conflicts!

Resolving Internal Conflict

The overriding ambition of an organization's endeavors should be to maximize its return on capital employed as a whole. It is vital that managers responsible for taking decisions about transfer pricing cotton on to the importance of the organization's interests and understand that it is not necessary for each division to earn the same return, either by reference to sales or the level of investment. Any attempt by a divisional manager to increase his own division's returns at the expense of another division will lead to suboptimization and work against the fundamental purpose of the organization.

Think!
Does this sort of thing happen in your organization? What do you do to overcome it?

Unfortunately, unless the calculation of transfer prices is integrated into the organizational planning and budgeting system, and unless managers are fully aware of their activities on other divisions and on the attainment of the short- and long-term objectives of the organization, there will be an inevitable tendency to act in divisional interests. If the determination of transfer prices causes so much difficulty, why do we bother at all? Put simply, the abolition of transfer prices would fail to provide divisional managers with the appropriate economic base and incentive for correct decision making. This, in turn, prevents the meaningful measurement of performance of individual operating divisions.

Under these circumstances, it may be appropriate to consider dual transfer prices. This involves charging the buying division the lowest price it can obtain from external sources and crediting the selling division at a price that allows for a normal profit margin. The difference is subsidized by the parent organization to encourage both divisions to participate in the transfer. Such an approach should maximize returns to the organization as a whole as well as providing for a fair evaluation of the selling division's performance and motivating the manager of the buying division to make optimal short-term decisions.

What's Really Important?

In looking for an answer to this question, we need to look at both internal and external interactions for each has a significant impact on how we may utilize transfer pricing to maximize returns for the organization. Here, we shall focus on the important internal issues and leave discussion on the external situation until a later chapter.

Multidivisional organizations have a particular need for a system that draws together the disparate and diverse elements within the group and to ensure the proper pursuit of their long-run objectives. Transfer pricing policies, practices, and techniques must form an integral part of that system for, as we have already seen, transfer pricing commands a vital role in interdivisional relations. At the same time, transfer pricing assists in the process of allocating scarce resources, which it does by breaking the tendency to suboptimize. So, what do we need to focus on?

Let me start by making an explicit statement: The transfer pricing method used must generate a competitive price in a spirit of fairness and realism. This concept is central to the whole notion of decentralization, which is the cornerstone of multidivisional organizations. In these organizations, returns (on either capital employed or sales or both) are the more commonly used yardsticks for the measurement of managerial effectiveness and if transfer prices are not competitive, an important tool in management evaluation is lost.

The organization's transfer pricing system must therefore be realistic and lead to prices that will foster a healthy spirit of competition between divisions. Such a system will also provide an adequate yardstick against which divisional managers may be judged, and provide reliable financial information for central management decision making. These are perhaps the most important internal issues for transfer pricing is one of the available tools that multidivisional organizations may use to achieve a strategic competitive advantage.

Management Reporting

So far in this chapter, we have looked at the management issues that surround the topic of transfer pricing. The one thing we have not really considered up to now is how an organization should actually deal with the complete transfer pricing process, which presents a formidable challenge. Specifically, they seek to solve the problem of achieving a transfer pricing system that:

- satisfies the needs of the organization with respect to strategy and internal incentives;
- results in an efficient use of resources; and
- provides the *right* transfer pricing answer from the perspective of the various revenue authorities.

What we need is a reporting system that will help us understand the organization's performance in these key areas. Unfortunately, a familiar problem with developing most management-reporting systems is that the data generally available, which are required to complete the organization's annual report, tax returns, and reports to regulatory agencies and other outside constituencies, may not be detailed enough or in a suitable format to conduct the sorts of analyses that are used internally by management to evaluate the organization and its constituent divisions, and to adjust its strategic direction.

Think!

Does this sound familiar? Is your management information system capable of providing the sort of information needed to solve this thorny problem of transfer pricing?

From the perspective of our transfer pricing system, the development of a useful management reporting system often faces hurdles related to key analytical issues, such as:

- the attribution of organizational overheads to individual divisions;
- distinguishing between the relevant variable costs attributable to internal and external sales; and
- reporting individual divisional, and aggregated organizational, performance in such a way that we understand the effectiveness of transfer pricing activities.

In most cases, these analytical challenges are solvable in many different ways, each of which is likely to have drawbacks of its own and is probably not demonstrably superior in all situations. Understanding that our management-reporting system is critical for evaluating the performance of the organization as well as its divisional managers, the system we create to manage our transfer pricing process needs to provide information that confirms or refutes our ability to achieve the aims attributed to our transfer pricing system.

At the same time, we must understand that the data generated are quite often key determinants of employee compensation, such as the establishment of bonus payments. This increases the importance of developing a mechanism that attributes portions of the revenue streams earned by a given product, or service, to the various divisions involved in its development, construction, and distribution. In a similar fashion, the expenses incurred by various organizational cost centers, such as product development, organizational marketing, information technology, and back-office operations, must also be attributed to the various divisions being credited with the revenues from the products with which these expenses are associated. So, from every perspective, it is important that we get it right.

Reporting for management is a complex and often thankless task. Each manager requires something different but this should be expected in the diverse ecosystem that is a multidivisional or multinational organization. As you have seen, there are many things that we must consider when developing a transfer pricing performance–reporting system, but most of all, it should emphasize our organization's strategy in this area and the key initiatives chosen to achieve it. Choosing the most appropriate performance measures will help everyone see more clearly how transfer pricing activities contribute to overall organizational performance. Traditional reporting and performance-measurement systems are becoming less fashionable as they rarely approach this vital activity in a strategic, forward-thinking way. Strategy mapping and scorecarding are the way of the future.

Performance Measurement

Generally, our performance-measurement system tells us whether we are on the way to reaching our strategic objectives. These will change from time to time to reflect changes in the world in which we operate. This means that our performance-measurement system should be in a state of constant review that will probably result in frequent changes to ensure it remains aligned with our strategic objectives. Failure to do this will cause employees to continue to reflect on things that are now less important while not focusing on what is newly important. Since we only comprehend what we measure, our organization's inertia will keep it moving in the same direction it had been going should we fail to change measurements. This is equally true of the performance-measurement system we develop for our transfer pricing activities.

Numerous performance measures dilute our attention from the things that matter. We need to identify several key indicators that will articulate what it is that we need to get better at if we are going to optimize our overall organizational performance. Importantly, in the process of determining transfer pricing policy, some things have a greater effect than others and so we must explicitly specify the relative weights for each indicator when they are used to assess performance. As you can see, it is important that performance measurement reflects our strategic direction

Think!

How good is your performance-measurement system? Does it focus on the things that really matter? Does it change as circumstances change?

and that the reporting of performance properly compares actual achievement with the intention of our transfer pricing strategy.

A well-designed performance-reporting system focuses on results and measures these results against objectives and targets that have already been established. How well these results measure up is a key element in evaluating our chances of reaching our destination. What is more, it will have everyone pulling in the same direction, since we are all working toward the same objectives. Unfortunately, for any organization, a good reporting system will not turn a poor performance into a good performance. However, it may turn a good performance into an even better performance because the information provided encourages individual divisions to strive for the best.

Summary

An organization's financial objectives are important considerations in the development of a transfer pricing policy. Meeting them will only be possible if income is derived in the division where the cash flow is ultimately required. Also, if our transfer pricing system is to operate correctly, it must accurately reflect the economics of the interaction between the trading partners. Transfer pricing methods that have been used in the past, and quite probably are still being used, are often based on an overly simplified model of how commercial organizations operate.

While up until now, these oversimplified models may not have done a bad job of maximizing the wealth of owners, the increasing complication of commercial activities that cross jurisdictional boundaries means that we need to reexamine our transfer pricing policy. It is in our organization's interests that the revised policy is acceptable under the generally recognized OECD principles. Of course, a transfer pricing policy cannot be established, set in stone, and then ignored. If it is to have any value, the policy we develop should be responsive to an increasingly dynamic and volatile business and regulatory environment and ought to be reviewed, and refined where necessary, on a regular and frequent basis. The best time for this is during the routine process of reviewing the overall organizational strategy.

Inevitably, this is likely to require a change in management thought about the arrangement of functions, risks, and intangibles within divisions of the organization. As long as the proposed changes, particularly with regard to pricing and profit, continue to reflect the substance of each transaction, placing functions, risks, and intangibles in divisions that allow us to increase the owners' wealth should be pursued with vigor. Such changes, however, will often lead to a considerable range of problems. Once we have decided exactly what changes to make to our transfer pricing policy, we must also communicate the rationale of the changes to all those involved, ensure that the new policy is implemented smoothly, and put in place a monitoring system that will allow us to attribute the effect of each of the changes on both divisional and overall profitability.

CHAPTER 3

External Influences on Transfer Pricing

Introduction

Not that long ago, transfer pricing was a subject for tax administrators and one or two other specialists. But, more recently, businesspeople, economists, and politicians, as well as a number of nongovernmental organizations, have been waking up to the importance of who pays tax, on what, and perhaps importantly where, on international business transactions between different arms of the same business enterprise. Globalization is one reason for this interest, and the rise of MNEs is another. Once you take on board the fact that more than 60% of world trade takes place within these MNEs, the importance of transfer pricing, both internally and externally, becomes clear.

Most of the time, transfer pricing is used to distribute overall profit between parts of an MNE group for tax minimization and other strategic purposes. Consider a profitable US computer supplier that buys microchips from its subsidiary in Korea. How much the US entity pays its subsidiary—the transfer price—will determine how much profit the Korean unit reports and how much local tax it pays. If the US entity pays below normal local-market prices, the Korean unit may appear to be in financial difficulty, even if collectively they show a decent profit margin when the completed computer is sold. The US Inland Revenue Service might not grumble as the profit will be reported at their end, but their Korean counterparts will be disappointed in not having as much profit, as perhaps they ought to tax on their side of the operation. This problem only arises inside business entities with operations in more than one country. If the US entity bought its microchips from an independent company in Korea, it would pay the market price, and the supplier would pay taxes on its own profits in the normal way.

Think!

Does your organization use transfer pricing for tax minimization or other strategic purposes? Does it cause friction at a business-unit level?

Clearly, when both parties to an international transaction are under some form of common control, the revenue authorities in both countries may consider that the transaction price is not subject to the full play of market forces. Perceiving this to be designed by the controlling entity to pay less tax, in total, than it would under normal circumstances, interest of the revenue authorities in the transaction is intensified. In this chapter, then, we'll look at the external influences that come into play when formulating a transfer pricing policy.

Attracting International Organizations

Foreign direct investment (FDI) has traditionally been considered as an organization from one country making a physical investment in property, plant, and equipment in another country. In recent years, as a result of the rapid growth and change in global investment patterns, our understanding of FDI has widened to include the acquisition of a lasting management interest in an enterprise outside the investing organization's home country. Consequently, this investment may take many forms, such as the establishment of a new operating facility in a host country, or establishing a joint venture or strategic alliance with a local organization, or even the acquisition of a host country–based organization.

The mode of investment aside, FDI plays an exceptional and growing role in global business. It provides organizations with an opportunity to establish facilities in other places that are either closer to key markets or offer lower operating costs, as well as providing access to new markets, products, skills, and technology, and alternative financing and marketing channels. For a host country, it provides a source of new capital, employment opportunities, process technology, products, and skills in addition to valuable foreign exchange, and as such can provide a strong impetus to economic development.

Reacting to the growing liberalization of national regulatory frameworks governing investment in enterprises, and changes in technology and capital markets, profound changes have occurred in the size, scope, and methods of FDI. It has come to play a major role in the globalization of commercial enterprises. For small- and medium-sized enterprises, FDI represents an opportunity to become more actively involved in international business activities. Yet, larger MNEs and conglomerates still undertake the overwhelming percentage of FDI. Whatever the size of an organization looking to make an FDI, new information technology systems and a decline in global communication costs have made management of foreign investments far easier than in the past.

The global sea change in trade and investment policies, particularly tariff liberalization, the easing of restrictions on foreign investment and acquisition in many countries, and the deregulation and privatization of many industries, has probably been the most significant catalyst for the expansion of FDI. The greatest effect has been seen in developing countries, where inward FDI flows increased from a yearly average of less than US$6 billion in the 1970s to a little more than US$20 billion in the 1980s. During the 1990s, yearly inward FDI flows to developing countries exploded from US$35 billion in 1990 to US$116 billion in 1995 and US$229 billion at the close of the last millennium. After the first 10 years of the 21st century, this has more than doubled to US$573 billion. Developing countries don't have a monopoly on these inward flows as, driven by mergers, acquisitions, and the global nature of production in a range of industries, FDI into developed countries was US$602 billion in 2010, which as a result of the global financial crisis is well below the peak of US$1,307 billion in 2007.[1]

Think!

Is your organization one of the contributors to this explosion? Has it really been of benefit?

Proponents of FDI point out that the exchange of investment flows benefits both the home country and the host country. Opponents, however, note that the largest of MNEs are able to wield great power over smaller and weaker economies and can drive out much local competition. As with every debate, the truth lies somewhere in the middle. Nevertheless, when an FDI is made in any foreign country, the strategic business objective is simple. It is to tap into a lucrative demand base and earn larger profits through strategies such as achieving economies of scale and growing market share. Such a commercial venture requires a high-risk investment in an unknown economy, which should be thought through very carefully if the possibility of profit repatriation is limited in any way.

There are, of course, many innovative ways to circumvent the restrictions on profit repatriations without getting into any legal trouble. One of the most common of these is by using transfer pricing. When purchase and sale contracts are signed between the parent MNE and its foreign operation, at trade terms that favor the parent, it results in profit repatriation. This kind of tilted transfer pricing, where the parent MNE licenses technology, or charges for services provided, to its foreign operation at inflated prices, allows for effective repatriation of profits to the parent MNE. Although there is nothing illegal about this practice, it is sure to raise the ire of the revenue authorities in the foreign country if the transfer prices used are completely out of line with the market rates or are blatantly overinflated. It provides a foundation for future conflict.

Government Income

Many governments, especially in industrialized and developed nations, pay very close attention to FDI because the investment flows into and out of their economies can and do have a significant impact. However, it is the post-investment transfers that are likely to have a greater impact with the areas most affected being the balance on the government account, the balance on the current account, and foreign currency reserves. In an open economy that is well supported by FDI, transfer pricing policies put in place by MNEs are likely to have an impact in each of these areas but it is the first, the balance on the government account, that is of most interest to us in the transfer pricing discussion. Let's look quickly at this to better understand why this is so.

Balance on the government account refers to the difference between government revenue and government expenditure. At present, primarily due to the global economic crisis, many governments are running a deficit, that is, they are spending more than they are bringing in. Here is not the place to engage in a debate about whether this is right or wrong but we do need to grasp the impact of FDI attraction on the government account. Let's start with the expenditure side of the equation. When a government is actively seeking inward FDI, it will look to offer a variety of incentives that range from many forms of direct subsidies to tax holidays and the creation of special tax-privileged zones. Quite obviously, subsidies increase government expenditure in the short term before the anticipated rewards, in the form of increased taxation revenue, are reaped.

Think!

In how many ways do your international trading activities impact on either your home or host nation's finances? Are you a net contributor or a net detractor from these?

On a positive note, the income side of the government account will grow as a result of the increase in economic activity brought about by inward FDI. One of the sources of this growth in income is personal income taxes and social security contributions from the additional employment created by inward FDI. On top of this, there is the profits tax payable as a result of this increase in economic activity. While this will be offset to a certain extent by any form of agreed reduction in the normal level of income tax payable by organizations involved in inward FDI, a more significant negative impact usually comes from the transfer pricing policies of those MNEs contributing to inward FDI.

For MNEs, transfer pricing is often a significant issue with much at stake. As a result, they have structured their transfer pricing policies in their own interests with little or no regard for those of their host or home governments. This has led to governments around the world suffering, for many years, a leakage of income as a result of these arrangements. Little by little, governments have introduced legislation to protect their income streams from price manipulation in the business activities of these large organizations. Typically, on transactions between two or more countries, the focus has been on forcing arm's-length pricing, that is, the price at which the transaction would take place between an independent buyer and seller, between the related organizations involved.

The global economic crisis has created a new momentum for change by providing a catalyst for concerted international action in areas like tax transparency, and tackling avoidance and evasion. Increasingly, as cash-strapped national governments look for stronger ways to protect their income streams, transfer pricing has become a much more significant area of focus for the taxing authorities as they seek to limit the transfer of profits and valuable income-earning assets from one jurisdiction to another, generally low-tax one.

These days, most governments align their transfer pricing legislation with the 2010 OECD guidelines. This, coupled with bilateral agreements between many major trading partners, is leading to increased consistency in how countries tax their resident MNEs' transfer pricing activities. These agreements establish rules for apportioning MNEs' income among the nations in which they conduct business. These rules attempt to tax all MNEs' income once, and only once, at a national level.[2] In other words, tax treaties attempt to avoid the double taxation that would occur if, as often happens, when there are transfer pricing–related adjustments made to assessable income by the taxing authority in one country; two nations tax the same income.

A Scenario for Conflict

The delicate balance between the interests of MNEs and their host or home governments is even more important than ever. Transfer pricing is one crucial area where it is essential that this balance is maintained. Frequent legislative changes and the differing regimes of jurisdictions continue to increase the burden of compliance for MNEs and provide fertile ground for conflict. Yet, I need to make it very clear that fractious relationships between MNEs and the taxing authorities are not the only source of conflict arising from transfer pricing policies. Figure 3.1 provides a graphic illustration of the extent of this policy conflict.

When related entities transfer products or services across jurisdictions, transfer prices play a role in the calculation of the entity's overall income tax liability. In this situation, the entity's transfer pricing policy can become a tax-planning tool. The United States has agreements with most other nations that determine how MNEs are to be taxed in the

Figure 3.1. Possible fractious relationships.

respective jurisdictions where they have operations. Since transfer prices represent revenue to the upstream entity and an expense to the downstream entity, the transfer price affects the calculation of entity profits that represent taxable income in the nations where they are based.

Think!
Have you experienced conflict in one or more of these transfer pricing relationships? How was it resolved?

For example, a pharmaceutical company manufactures a drug in a factory that it operates in Ireland and transfers the drug to its marketing entity in the United States for sale. A high transfer price increases the taxable income of the Irish entity, which obviously results in a higher tax liability in Ireland. At the same time, the high transfer price increases the cost of product to the US marketing division, which lowers its income leading to lower US taxes. The entity's incentive in using such a transfer pricing policy depends on whether its marginal tax rate is higher in the United States or in Ireland. If the marginal tax rate is higher in the United States, the entity prefers a high transfer price, whereas if the marginal tax rate is higher in Ireland, it will prefer a low transfer price. The general rule is that the entity will look to shift income from the high tax jurisdiction to the low tax jurisdiction.

There are limits to the extent to which companies can shift income in this manner. When a market price is available for the goods or services transferred, the taxing authorities will usually impose the market-based transfer price. When a market-based transfer price is simply not available, the tax law in many jurisdictions contains detailed and complicated rules that limit the extent to which companies can shift income out of their jurisdiction. For example, in Australia, transfer pricing rules are designed to ensure that the country receives an appropriate share of tax revenue from the international dealings of MNEs, reflecting contributions made by their Australian operations to the overall group's operating performance. These rules, intended to protect the integrity of the Australian tax system, have been introduced to ensure that its government revenue is not compromised and that consistency is maintained with its international tax treaty partners. Paradoxically, the operation of these rules is limited to cases where its application would result in greater tax receipts in Australia and discretely ignored should they result in a benefit to another country.

Transfer pricing often becomes relevant in the context of other regulatory issues, including international trade disputes. For example, when tariffs are based on the value of goods imported, the transfer price of goods shipped from a manufacturing division in one country to a marketing division in another country can form the basis for the tariff. As another example, in order to increase investment in their economies, developing nations sometimes restrict the extent to which multinational companies can repatriate profits. However, when a product is transferred from manufacturing divisions located elsewhere into the developing nation for sale, the local marketing division can export funds to "pay" for the merchandise received. As a final example, when nations accuse foreign companies of "dumping" product onto their markets, transfer pricing is often involved. Dumping refers to selling product below cost, and it generally violates international trade laws. Foreign companies frequently transfer products from manufacturing divisions in their home countries to marketing affiliates elsewhere, so that the determination of whether the company has dumped products depends on comparing the transfer price charged to the marketing affiliate with the upstream division's cost of delivering their product.

In theory, transfer pricing and customs rules seek to impose a similar standard on related-party pricing—prices should reflect those that would exist if the parties were unrelated. However, there is a long history of tension between tax and customs administrations. The relevant rules are governed by different international ruling bodies (the WTO for customs, the OECD for transfer pricing) and have different objectives. Tax administrations generally have an incentive to minimize the cost of goods sold and thus import prices. Conversely, customs administrations generally have an incentive to maximize the cost of goods sold and thus import prices, resulting in higher dutiable value and processing fees. Other differences include:

- different sets of regulations;
- different filing time periods (generally entry-by-entry for customs versus annual tax returns);
- different methods for determining an arm's-length price;
- different presumptions as to the key determinants of comparability (product/industry for customs versus functional equivalence for tax).

Transfer pricing rules suggest that a transaction between related organizations meets the arm's-length standard if the results of the transaction are consistent with the results that would have been realized if independent organizations had engaged in the same transaction under the same circumstances. In reaching this conclusion, the tax transfer pricing rules often look at not only the transaction itself but also at the various functions, such as research and development, manufacturing, sales, marketing, distribution, and services, such as back-office activities, which support each and every transaction.

The customs value of imported goods is generally its transaction value, which is the price actually paid or payable for the goods when sold for export to the country of importation, provided that the buyer and seller are not related. When they are related, the transaction value may be acceptable for customs purposes as long as the revenue authority in the receiving country is satisfied that the relationship did not influence the price.

The challenge for MNEs lies in reconciling these differences to achieve, support, and document an arm's-length result in a way that satisfies the general principles of both sets of rules. The clarification of transfer pricing rules and the use of effective transfer pricing planning are becoming more and more important if MNEs are to avoid double, or even multiple, taxation, which can limit the opportunity for economic growth through international trade.

The International Peacekeeper

Is it possible to find an arbiter to pour oil on troubled waters? If we think of all the international nongovernmental institutions that could be involved, we see that several have a direct interest in one side of the conflict or the other. As I mentioned earlier, the WTO is particularly interested in the trade aspects of transfer pricing, whereas the OECD is more keenly involved in the taxation aspects.

Perhaps, we could look to the World Bank, or the International Monetary Fund (IMF), to take on the role of a peacekeeper in this increasingly fractious situation. Looking at the latter, one of its objectives is to facilitate international trade. Yet, understandably, given the seemingly unending global economic crisis, their priorities are directed toward bringing some stability to, and the strengthening of, the international monetary system.

Returning then to the possibility of the World Bank taking on the role of a peacemaker, we can find evidence that they have not been disinterested in this policy conflict. In 2006, in conjunction with PricewaterhouseCoopers, they produced a report entitled *Paying Taxes: The Global Picture*[3] that provided a comparison of the world's tax regimes with the overall aim of encouraging improvements in the design of tax systems that would benefit all parties—businesses, governments, and tax authorities. It doesn't address the issue of transfer pricing specifically but the emphasis is on designing a system that considers the total tax contribution rather than the individual components such as profits tax and trade levies.

Clearly, these two organizations have bigger pictures to look at, which leaves us with a return to expecting the WTO and the OECD to work together to achieve some harmony in this perennial conflict. To this end, conferences held in 2006 and 2007 jointly between the World Customs Organization (WCO), a part of the WTO, and the OECD[4] have led to an increasing dialogue toward regulatory convergence in this regard. This dialogue focuses on the comparison of customs valuation and transfer pricing methods, as well as the desirability and feasibility of having converging standards for the two systems. Out of this dialogue, there appears to have emerged two schools of thought: those who view convergence of rules and regulation as desirable and feasible, and those who are cautious with this approach.

Those who are in favor of convergence point out that a credibility question is likely to arise if two sets of rules on value determination exist within one government, whereas those who are cautious about convergence point out that the two systems are based on different principles regarding the valuation of imported goods. Trade levies are determined by the customs authorities using the value of the goods based on information available at the time of importation with respect to individual transactions. On the other hand, the profits tax implication of transfer pricing activities is determined by the value of the goods based on information available at the year end with respect to aggregated transactions in an individual business as a whole.

Currently, the tax and customs authorities treat transfer pricing in accordance with different international standards, namely, the OECD Transfer Pricing Guidelines and the WTO Customs Valuation Agreement. There are many differences and similarities between the two sets of rules that are applied by tax and customs agencies to transfer pricing and it is acknowledged that much could be done to encourage converging standards and coordinated administrative approaches. In the latter area in particular, a greater degree of acceptability by one agency of a value determination by the other, the acceptance more generally of advance pricing agreements, the conduct of joint audits, understanding the consequences of a readjustment of the transfer price made by one agency on another, regular exchange of information, and cooperation between customs and tax agencies are all considered possible ways of avoiding conflict in the future.

Of course, one size does not fit all and engaging in such initiatives would mean a long road ahead because it would involve a comprehensive review of internal processes and systems by all three parties to the transfer pricing conundrum—customs, tax, and business.

Summary

There are now close to 200 separate nations in our world, although some are disputed, that all compete for a share of the economic wealth generation of commercial enterprises. They do so in a variety of ways and with varying degrees of success. With the government in a little more than one-quarter of these nations actually generating a positive balance on their current account, protecting what revenues they currently receive, as well as looking for ways to secure more, leads to increased concern over, and policing of, the transfer pricing activities of MNEs operating in their territory. Conflicts, many of which are minor, inevitably arise from this increased oversight and this will often result in a souring of previously sound relationships.

Looking at developments with a sense of balance, it would be fair to say that the vast majority of MNEs transact their business activities between related organizations in a responsible way. Nevertheless, there are a significant number of MNEs that, with just a passing regard to the underlying economics of a transaction, use transfer pricing as a means to maximize their profits in no doubt legal, but not necessarily moral, ways.

There is no doubt that more comparability between the OECD Transfer Pricing Guidelines and the WTO Customs Valuation Agreement, as well as their enhanced enforcement in cross-border-related party transactions, will go some way in assuaging the sources of conflict. However, it also needs to be said that MNEs also need to reflect on their role in this conflict and implement more responsible pricing of their cross-border activities that not only satisfy the obligation to their owners but also their social responsibility to those host nations that have provided them with the wherewithal to increase their overall wealth.

It is the search for ways to enhance the business element of transfer pricing that is the focus of the remainder of this book.

CHAPTER 4

Changes in the Business Model

Introduction

Organizations competing on an international basis face choices in terms of resource allocation, the balance of authority between the central office and business units, and the degree to which products and services are customized in order to accommodate tastes and preferences of local markets. These choices have historically resulted in MNEs adopting either a global or domestic business model with their associated strategies.

A global strategy involves a high degree of concentration of resources and capabilities in the central office and centralization of authority in order to exploit potential scale and learning economies. Customization at the local level is thus necessarily low.

A variable domestic strategy, on the other hand, reflects a contrary view. In this situation, resources are dispersed throughout the various countries where the organization does business, decision-making authority is pushed down to the local level, and each business unit is allowed to customize product and market offerings to specific needs. By adopting such a strategy, the MNE as a whole foregoes the benefits that could be derived from centralization and coordination of diverse activities in favor of potentially greater market share leading to increased profitability at the local level.

In truth, neither of these strategies on their own will be successful in the business world of the 21st century—a business world that is moving from a primarily vertical system for creating value to a more horizontal value-creation model. Indeed, Sir John Rose, former CEO of Rolls-Royce plc, whose company services customers in more than 120 countries through a global network of research, service, and manufacturing workers was very clear about this. In the United Kingdom, Rolls-Royce plc is considered a British company but in the United States they are an

American company, in Singapore, they are a Singaporean company, and in Germany, they are a German company.[1] So much so that he was once asked to accompany German Chancellor Schroeder on a visit to Russia to secure business for German companies.[2] They are truly a transnational corporation.

Just what is meant by a transnational corporation? It is an MNE that embraces a model that represents a compromise between local autonomy and centralized decision making. In so doing, the organization seeks a balance between the pressures for global integration and the pressures for local responsiveness. It achieves this balance by pursuing a distributed strategy that is a hybrid of the centralized and decentralized strategies.

The Transnational Organization

When employing a transnational strategy, the goal is to combine elements of global and multi-domestic strategies. A transnational strategy allows for the attainment of benefits inherent in both global and multi-domestic strategies. The overseas components are integrated into the overall corporate structure across several dimensions, and each of the components is empowered to become a source of specialized innovation. It is a management approach in which an organization integrates its global business activities through close cooperation and interdependence among its headquarters, operations, and international subsidiaries, and its use of appropriate global information technologies.

The key philosophy of a transnational organization is adaptation to all environmental situations and achieving flexibility by capitalizing on multidirectional knowledge flows in the form of decision reasoning and value-added information, and two-way communication throughout the organization. The principal characteristic of a transnational strategy is the differentiated contributions by all its units to integrated worldwide operations. As one of its other characteristics, a joint innovation by headquarters and by some of the overseas units leads to the development of relatively standardized and yet flexible products and services that can capture several local markets. Such an approach means that decision making and knowledge generation are distributed among every unit of a transnational organization.

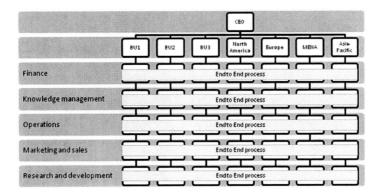

Figure 4.1. An example of a transnational organizational structure.

Utilizing the old adage that structure follows strategy, any transnational strategy must be supported by an appropriate structure in order to effectively implement the strategy. Just as the transnational strategy is a combination, or hybrid strategy, between global and multi-domestic strategies, the organizational structure of firms pursuing transnational strategies is a matrix one that draws on characteristics of the worldwide geographic structure, the worldwide product divisional structure and the worldwide support structure as depicted in Figure 4.1. The combination of mechanisms needed is somewhat contradictory, because the structure needs to be centralized and decentralized, integrated and nonintegrated, and formalized and nonformalized. But organizations that can successfully implement this strategy and structure often perform better than those pursuing only multi-domestic or global strategies.

A transnational model represents a compromise between local autonomy and centralized decision making. The organization seeks a balance between the pressures for global integration and the pressures for local responsiveness. It achieves this balance by pursuing a distributed strategy, which is a hybrid of the centralized and decentralized strategies. Under the transnational model, an MNE's assets and capabilities are dispersed according to the most beneficial location for a specific activity. Simultaneously, overseas operations are interdependent, and knowledge is developed jointly and shared worldwide.

Think!

How would you categorize your organization? Is it simply an MNE or would you consider it to be transnational?

One organization that appears to be successfully implementing a transnational strategy by making centralization decisions based partly on whether value-chain activities are upstream or downstream is Nestlé. During an interview with Suzy Wetlaufer, Nestlé's Chairman and former CEO, Peter Brabeck was sure that "the closer we come to the consumer, in branding, pricing, communication, and product adaptation, the more we decentralize. The more we are dealing with production, logistics, and supply-chain management, the more centralized decision making becomes. After all, we want to leverage Nestlé's size, not be hampered by it."[3]

From this simple understanding of a transnational organization, it is clear that they are prime candidates to suffer significant transfer pricing conflict. Furthermore, policy statements or pricing models, or perhaps even both, need to be embedded in their business strategy to limit the possibility of conflicts that are likely to have a significant detrimental effect on organizational performance.

Business Strategy

In the context of transfer pricing, much time and effort are spent on discussion of supply-chain issues that relate to property transactions, both tangible and intangible. Tracking how expenditure flows through the organization, from the initial purchase order in procurement through the incoming–conversion–outgoing process and ultimately to the receipt of payment from the end customer is not easy. It is often impossible, almost always expensive but absolutely essential if any organization, whether an MNE or a transnational organization, is to steer clear of transfer pricing conflict.

It is no wonder then that little effort is directed toward understanding the impact of the outsourcing of information technology, headquarters activities, and other services that have become really important in recent years. This outsourcing almost always creates transfer pricing issues because there is rarely any market-based information against which an organization can benchmark.

On reflection, at present, for many MNEs and transnational organizations, the transfer pricing policy component of their business strategy considers the following points that were discussed in Chapter 2:

- Management of competitive pressures;
- Movement of funds between related organizations;
- Repatriation of profits;
- Managing the effects of asymmetry in exchange rates; and
- Reducing the impact of taxes and tariffs.

Why have these been considered key points in developing a transfer pricing policy? For starters, MNEs are in a position to utilize their presence in different countries, especially low-cost ones, to lower input costs through structured transfer pricing so that they can match, or undercut, local competition in the supply of finished product. Next, for political or other reasons, MNEs may prefer to invest funds in one country rather than another. Transfer pricing provides an indirect way of shifting funds into, or out of, a particular country. While trying to achieve these specific objectives, disputes are likely to arise between the MNEs and the revenue authorities in the relevant countries, resulting in a reduction in overall organizational effectiveness and profitability. Something to avoid at all times!

For MNEs, one of the biggest risk exposures is their balances of various foreign currencies. Through astute management, MNEs are able to structure transfer pricing arrangements in such a way as to mitigate their exposure to fluctuating foreign exchange relationships. This is not such a bad thing but the management of foreign exchange exposures for an MNE is a relatively complex centralized function, the costs of which need to be considered in any transfer pricing model.

Perhaps, the most common use of transfer pricing, and probably the foundation of many an MNEs' transfer pricing policies, is to reduce their overall tax liability. The objective is to maximize profits in countries where the tax burden is lower, thus reducing the tax expense of the organization as a whole. Yet, there is another side to this coin where product transfers are concerned and that is the tariffs that will be payable on the imported goods, which sometimes are considerable. As I mentioned earlier in the book, this interplay provides fertile ground for conflict, which creates a serious side issue that takes the organization's managers' eyes off the main game—that of maximizing the return to the owners of the enterprise.

Perhaps a more realistic starting point for the transfer pricing policy component of business strategy should be to create a foundation grounded in the OECD's international transfer pricing standard. This standard is predicated on the concept that transactions between independent parties are conducted at prices determined by market forces. Yet, those market forces are not always present in transactions between related parties. Perhaps, the best example of this is the possibility of a bad debt arising as a result of a sale transaction. While that is always a possibility in a normal commercial transaction, it is highly unlikely in a transaction between related parties and so some allowance for that needs to be made in the pricing of a related-party transaction.

In a bid to avoid debate over issues such as this, current OECD transfer pricing guidelines are based on the arm's-length principle, that is, a transfer price should be the same as if the two companies involved were indeed two independents and not part of the same organizational structure. The arm's-length principle is found in Article 9 of the OECD Model Tax Convention and is the framework for bilateral treaties between OECD countries and many non-OECD governments too. The OECD Transfer Pricing Guidelines, in helping MNEs avoid double taxation and tax administrations to receive a fair share of the tax base of those same MNEs, provide a framework for settling such matters by providing considerable detail as to how to apply the arm's-length principle. But all of this assumes the best possible world, where tax authorities and MNEs work together in good faith—not always a realistic situation.

Applying transfer pricing rules based on the arm's-length principle is not easy, even with the help of the OECD's guidelines. It is not always possible, and often takes valuable time, to find comparable market transactions on which the individual business units within an MNE are able to set an acceptable transfer price. What is the alternative? As I mentioned earlier in the book, the OECD guidelines provide several alternatives, such as the comparable uncontrolled price method, the resale price method, the cost plus method, the transactional net margin method, and the transactional profit split method, which could be used when the arm's-length principle just isn't feasible. Without recommending any one in favor of the others, they suggest that the most appropriate method should be used in any particular case. Unfortunately, these replacement systems are considered extremely complex to administer and likely to create discord with the revenue authorities in one or other, or even both of the countries involved in any given transaction.

The most frequently advocated alternative to the arm's-length principle is some kind of formula-based apportionment that would split the entire profits of an MNE among all of its business units regardless of their location. Such a worldwide taxing system has been a discussion topic for many years but it has never received international acclaim because the use of a formula inevitably results in winners and losers in the apportionment process. Of particular concern are those contentious areas such as head office costs, research and development expenditures, and the use of intellectual capital.

Think!

If you are engaged in transfer pricing activities, how do you determine the transfer prices? Do you opt for simplicity or detail?

As a generalization, the arm's-length principle avoids these pitfalls as it is based on individual transactions in real markets. It is tried and tested, offering MNEs and governments a single international standard for transfer pricing that gives different governments a fair share of the tax base of MNEs in their jurisdiction while avoiding double-taxation problems. Unquestionably, it is probably a good idea that this is the starting point for developing an organization's transfer pricing policy. Yet, if we look at the woods rather than the trees, the bigger problem lies in the determination of prices more generally and this is why, when we start to deconstruct our selling prices to independent third parties as part of the process for establishing transfer prices, difficulties are often encountered with the revenue authorities.

In the next chapter, I'll return to this discussion in more depth as part of the development of a transfer pricing model for the changing times. For now, I'd like to consider three things that should be reflected in the development of the transfer pricing policy component of business strategy—a reflection on how we should be using transfer pricing to create value for our owners, whether it is possible for our performance to be verified, and how we should communicate our efforts to our stakeholders.

The Notion of Added Value

We have established that the purpose of engaging in transfer pricing activities is to generate additional value for the owners of our MNE or transnational organization. How do we know if we have done that? Unfortunately, traditional accounting-based measures of operational performance focus on sales and profit increases, not on value generation and so they are really inappropriate for understanding whether our transfer pricing activities have been successful in generating wealth.

Given that value generation is the key driver of our success in transfer pricing, we should look to the use of economic value added, or EVA®, as a key performance measure. This metric is a refinement of the economic profit approach developed and trademarked by the New York management consultancy firm, *Stern, Stewart and Company.*

The economic profit approach has a long history and is widely used as a performance indicator because it reflects the notion that, for an organization to be profitable in an economic sense, it must generate returns that exceed those required by investors. It is not enough simply to make an accounting profit because this in no way represents required investor returns.

EVA® is a measure of the extent to which, if at all, the after-tax operating profit on one or more of our activities, exceeds the required minimum profit, which in turn is based on the investors' minimum required rate of return—their weighted average cost of capital (WACC)—on their investment multiplied by that investment. The formula is:

EVA® = Net operating profit after tax—(WACC × capital invested)

If there is an excess of actual profit over the required minimum, economic value will have been added and the owners will be wealthier. If there is a shortfall, the owners will be less wealthy because they will not have earned the return they expected, given the amount of investment and the required rate of return.

It would seem that this is a much more acceptable way of determining the success or otherwise of our transfer pricing policy. Yet, there are some hurdles to overcome before we are in a position to use such a performance measure. Perhaps, the most important of these is understanding the amount of investment attached to a particular transfer pricing activity. Is it identifiable? What do we have to do to isolate the individual elements of the investment?

On reflection, the answer to these questions is not much different from our understanding of the cost of things. How do we share common costs among the products or services that we sell? How reasonable is our allocation process? These are all valid questions and ones that I shall attempt to address in the final chapter of this book as part of the task of designing a transfer pricing model for the changing times.

The Ability to Audit

Accelerating change has characterized the business landscape for many years now and nowhere is this more evident than in the expansion of MNE activity and the emergence of the transnational organization. This significant growth has led to increased surveillance of their transfer pricing activities by the revenue authorities in the countries in which they operate. This activity will only continue as global economies become increasingly integrated, as cost structures change with increasing frequency, and we become overwhelmed with regulation.

Managers will need considered advice on more topics and more frequently than before. This role most likely will fall to the internal auditor and, for MNEs and transnational organizations in particular, the risks associated with and the regulatory compliance of transfer pricing activities will fall more and more under the spotlight. In its value preservation role, the internal auditor should be charged with verifying the transfer pricing calculations to ensure that they continue to add value to the organization while at the same time continue to comply with the differing regulations imposed by those nations where we are engaging in related business activities.

Think!

Do you have internal auditors in your organization? If so, are they responsible for confirming that transfer prices add value and comply with regulation?

In addition to this, managers will want some assurance that implementation of the organization's strategic objectives is occurring. To this end, the model that we develop for transfer pricing in the future needs to be verifiable and supportable in the context of organizational strategic objectives and government regulation.

Reporting to Stakeholders

It is all very well to look for new ways of effective transfer pricing but we do need to understand whether we are achieving the goals we set ourselves in this crucial aspect of fulfilling our strategy. In MNEs and transnational organizations, it is the strategic decisions in respect of transfer pricing that will influence the success or failure of our international ventures and, for this reason, they are some of the most important decisions we shall make. It follows that the value of information is potentially higher in relation to strategic decision making since the cost of mistakes is so much greater and so the importance of providing relevant and timely performance-related information should not be underestimated. Internal performance reports of different hues are a crucial ingredient in helping us here.

Naturally, various measurement criteria may be adopted but the important performance indicators are those that identify the degree of achievement of our transfer pricing objectives. Part of this is acknowledging that creating, understanding, impacting, managing, serving, manipulating, and exploiting markets are the common denominators of organizational strategy, which is nothing without implementation. There are two key elements in the drive for profitability. One is the ability to maximize revenues and the other is to reduce or contain costs. In relation to the first, a vital feature of our success is the ability to position our products, or services, within the market place in a way that generates an acceptable and sustainable profit margin. For MNEs and transnational organizations, a crucial element here is recognition of the role played by their transfer pricing policy. It impacts on the likelihood of being able to maintain high levels of profitability, the probability of competitive attack from other organizations, and the linkage with necessary operational improvement strategies to reduce or contain costs.

A well-designed performance-reporting system focuses on results and measures these results against objectives and targets that have already been established. To discover whether we have a good performance-reporting system, a number of questions need to be asked. First, are the reports being read and acted upon? Reports distributed without any feedback are an indication that the system is not highly effective. Indeed, they may not contain information that is relevant at the time. Second, do the reports provide sufficient information for us to take corrective action where necessary without delay? Internally, the main purpose of performance reporting is not to tell us where we have been but, more importantly, where we are going. If this kind of information can't be gathered from the reports, then they are simply not doing their job. Third, are we receiving the information we need in a timely fashion? Knowing we have problem days, or sometimes weeks, after it first becomes apparent simply isn't good enough.

Think!

Do you report specifically on transfer pricing activities in your organization? If so, does the reporting process meet these criteria?

We are well endowed with technology these days to ensure our performance reporting is online and real-time. Unfortunately, when it comes to our organization, a good reporting system will not turn a poor performer into a good performer. However, it may turn a good performer into an even better performer because the information provided encourages people to strive for the best.

This means that we must have suitable measures in place, which must reflect the core values of our organization with regard to transfer pricing. More importantly, the monitoring and reporting mechanisms we use should be designed to focus the behavior of all those involved on the journey toward achieving our objectives. The resulting common sense of direction fosters the necessary team effort required to produce the best possible outcomes.

Summary

Transfer prices are useful in several ways. They can help an MNE identify those parts of the organization that are performing well and not so well, and without proper transfer pricing, an MNE could suffer double taxation on the same profits. Yet, determining transfer prices causes so much difficulty and is so surrounded by snags. If this is the case, why are such prices necessary?

It could be argued that they are not really necessary in a vertically integrated organization, but when this integration crosses national borders, the failure to have justified transfer prices for a wide range of activities in such an organization will lead to significant conflict. In addition, the abolition of transfer prices would prevent the meaningful measurement of operating performance of individual operating units within the MNE or transnational organization. It would also prevent the accurate estimation of likely earnings on proposed investment projects. Furthermore, transfer prices give business-unit managers an economic base and incentive for correct decision making. Finally, without an acceptable transfer pricing mechanism, the very existence of our MNEs and transnational organizations would be at risk.

That said, because of a lack of pertinent data, there are still many instances in which the chosen transfer price cannot be justified on any logical grounds. On other occasions, managers are influenced by a variety of factors other than economic considerations. Many senior-management groups in MNEs and transnational organizations are unaware that suboptimizing behavior is occurring in their organizations or that a change in transfer pricing policies could markedly improve their overall group performance. Transfer pricing is an integral part of the operating system for MNEs and transnational organizations but there are many issues that need to be addressed. The scope for a modern transfer pricing system that not only enhances overall organizational performance but also avoids intense conflict is considerable.

CHAPTER 5

A Transfer Pricing Model for the Changing Times

Introduction

Back in Chapter 1, I talked about the need to know the cost of things. How we go about that is not overly important as long as we have a consistent approach that is relevant for our organization. Accuracy is not a key factor either. We just need to make sure that we understand the cost of making a product or service available to each of our customers, both external and internal, accurate to within 5% or 10%, and we should be on the right track to avoid transfer pricing conflicts. What is essential though is that we properly understand the cost of the item being transferred, for if we don't, we shall make the wrong decisions, which in the regulated transfer pricing arena could prove to be costly.

Understanding our costs is becoming an increasingly complex affair because, as a consequence of the spread of globalization, the foundations of many economies, as well as organizations, have shifted from an industrial base to a service and knowledge base. This shift is rapidly occurring around the world and, as a result, the importance of physical and financial assets in the business activities of organizations, especially MNEs and transnationals, is diminishing. Intangible assets are becoming the main drivers of performance and, as a result, represent a more significant element in the determination of transfer prices.

Accepting that successful managers must be able to focus their attention on factors that are critical in establishing and maintaining their competitive edge, managing these vital intangible assets, especially intellectual assets such as human capital, structural capital, customer capital, and business partner (or economic web) capital, as well as understanding how they contribute the delivery cost of products and services has become a serious challenge for managers. In the context of transfer pricing, what is needed is a disciplined approach to identify the application of all of these intellectual assets, both explicit and implicit, such that they are used to create economic value for an organization.

For MNEs and transnationals to enjoy a benign tax environment, validated transfer prices are one of the most critical success factors. This validation is not just about understanding costs. It also requires quantification of all of the assets applied to each transaction so that an adequate return can be factored into the price. But transfer pricing is more than a tax issue. It is also used for other purposes such as motivating good decisions and providing information for the sensible evaluation of managers and organizations alike. Looked at in this way, transfer pricing principles are applicable to every intra-family transaction in an organization. This includes not only transactions between head office and subsidiaries or branches, but also transactions among departments and among process owners, hierarchy, and even individuals.

It would seem then that the task in this chapter is to develop a transfer pricing model that not only includes the identifiable costs but also the cost of utilizing every asset, whether that is financial, physical, or intellectual, that is instrumental in each transaction. A transfer pricing model built in this way not only provides an avenue for validated transfer prices but it also becomes a useful managerial tool allowing managers to use transfer pricing as a driver for value creation in their business unit.

Developing the Model

Earlier in the book, I made an explicit statement, which was that the transfer pricing method used must generate a competitive price in a spirit of fairness and realism. Therefore, everything that is proposed in the dialogue that follows is directed toward achieving this. So, where do we begin? In building our model, there are two primary components in the determination of a transfer price. The first of these is the identifiable cost and the second is the return on those assets used in each transaction. Let's start our development with the cost component.

Understanding the Cost of Things

I think I should preface this section with a general health warning. It would be very easy, in our attempt to better understand the cost of things, to drill down through succeeding levels of business activity in our attempt to be certain of the right answer. That's not a sensible approach for it will require us to put in place systems that increase bureaucracy, and therefore cost, within our organization. As I have said before in this book, when it comes to understanding the cost of something, accuracy is not that important. It is far better for us to have reliable information that is approximately right, say 90% or better, than being precisely wrong.

For all transfer pricing activities, one of the key essentials is knowing what makes up the total cost of each of the products or services we are selling to related departments or organizations. This will be made up of two different cost types. There are those costs that relate directly to the product or service that we are providing and those costs that maintain our support functions, associated with both delivering the product or service to the customer and to the continuing interaction with that customer.

When trying to understand the cost of a particular product or service, the first of these, the direct cost, is easy to determine because it is directly identifiable with the product or service that we are providing. For example, in a law firm, when a lawyer gives advice to a client, the cost is easily determined by taking the amount of time spent and multiplying that by the lawyer's hourly rate. The second, the support cost, is more problematic. Usually, these costs are not readily identifiable with a particular product or service and so we have to try and understand what portion of them is associated with the product or service we are trying to price. In the example just used, how might we go about sharing the cost of the janitor, the secretary, or the office rent of our law firm to the individual services that we have provided to our clients?

Since it is imperative, in the longer term, that we recover all of our costs to remain profitable, it is important that we have some mechanism to allocate these support costs to the products or services that we sell in order to calculate the full cost. This process of allocation is a significant problem for many organizations because it is not easy to understand how much of their indirect costs are consumed by individual products or services. If it was understandable, then we would probably consider them to be directly identifiable costs and our problem would go away.

Unfortunately, whatever arbitrary allocation of support costs we choose to use often results in misleading information about product or service profitability. From a transfer pricing perspective, use of unreliable allocation methods is likely to result in both the suboptimization of resources within the organization as a whole and conflict with the revenue authorities in either or both of the supplying and receiving jurisdictions.

Given that we need to understand the total cost of our product or service, we shall always have a need to allocate some support costs. How should we go about that? Traditionally, the most common methods of allocating these support costs have been on the basis of a relevant direct input such as labor hours, or machine hours, or units of material. Old traditions die hard but the nature of our competitive environment is changing rapidly and the ways of old are proving insufficiently flexible to deal with the complexity encountered in our modern organizations.

So what are our choices? There are, of course, the long-established marginal and absorption costing systems available to us. For transfer pricing purposes, the first of these would not be acceptable because it does not provide the necessary total cost of the product or service. The second would work but it is likely that the total cost determined using this system would not satisfy even our relaxed accuracy requirements. There is an even better option available to us.

One of the most significant advances in costing methodology in recent times has been the introduction of activity-based costing (ABC). It is generally accepted that this costing system overcomes the shortcomings of the more traditional costing systems by providing more accurate ways of assigning the costs of support resources. In so doing, ABC provides a truer picture of what our products, processes, and customers really cost. As with most benefits, this comes at a cost with critics arguing that the task of determining cost drivers is too complicated and time consuming and the cost involved far outweighs any benefits that might be derived from improved cost allocation. While there are situations where this may have some merit, we must acknowledge that an effective and acceptable transfer pricing system requires the level of improved cost allocation provided by a well-thought-out ABC system.

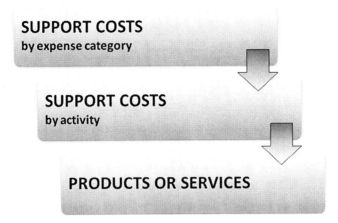

Figure 5.1. Activity-based costing model.

Since it will always be the activities our organization undertakes that drive its costs, it is these that we must focus on if we are to have the best possible transfer pricing system. Figure 5.1 shows the process by which ABC explains how activities consume resources and how products, services, or customers trigger activities. This provides a sound basis for our transfer pricing system as it identifies the causes (activities) and then the effects (costs) associated with each of the products or services for which we need a transfer price and puts our organization in a better position to justify the established transfer price to the relevant authorities. Having decided on the basis of understanding costs, let's move on to the more complex return on assets component.

Return on Assets Employed

Considering its importance, let's now understand how the return on assets employed is to be calculated and incorporated into the transfer pricing model. The very simple approach of determining the required return on the assets of the organization as a whole, and then allocating some portion of it to individual transfer pricing activities will not suffice because each transaction utilizes a different quantum of the individual categories of assets, that is, financial, physical, and intellectual assets.

The need to look at each category of asset individually, while it requires a more complex model, is really necessary and when we consider our transfer pricing requirements, adding an appropriate amount for each category to individual transfer prices will not only facilitate justification to the revenue authorities but also provide us with a more useful management decision tool. How then will we go about determining the utilization of, and subsequent required return on, each category, and indeed, in places, subcategories, of assets? Perhaps, the easiest way to work through this is to consider each category and subcategory of the asset in turn.

Financial Assets

It is rare that we have anything to consider in this category. It is not often that we tie up financial assets in any of our transfer pricing activities. Oh sure, we consume them to pay for direct inputs, support services, and the acquisition of other categories of assets but this is factored into our transfer pricing model in other ways. There is one situation, however, where we need to include an allowance for assets of this kind and that is when we provide a surety, that is a sum of money deposited as a guarantee against non-fulfillment of our obligations, for a particular transaction or activity. When it relates to a single transaction, the inclusion of an amount for the required return on the asset in the transfer pricing calculation is straightforward. We simply add the calculated required return to the transfer price. On the other hand, if a number of individual pricing calculations are included in a particular activity, then we need to allocate the required return to each of the transfer prices based on the cause(s) that trigger the need for the surety.

Physical Assets

This is perhaps the easiest of the asset categories to assess because the monetary information is readily available. There are two subcategories to consider, which are property, plant and equipment (PPE), and working capital. Starting with PPE, we encounter a similar problem to that experienced with support costs earlier in that we need to understand how these assets are used in each of our transfer pricing activities. There's no reason, then, why we should not adopt a similar approach to solving the problem. Indeed, in the process of understanding the cost of a particular transfer pricing activity, we may already have the solution. Let me explain: When we are trying to understand the cost of things, one of the factors we must consider is how much of our PPE is consumed in completing the activity. If we know this amount for each activity in relation to the total amount, then we can use the same ratio to determine how much of the required return on any given asset needs to be allocated to each transfer-price calculation.

We can approach the determination of return on assets in the case of our investment in working capital in much the same way. First, let's be clear about what we mean by working capital. In usual management parlance, working capital includes three elements—inventory, accounts receivable, and accounts payable. The first two of these are assets and so we need to include an allowance in our transfer pricing calculation for the required return on the investment in inventory and accounts receivable for each transaction. On the other hand, accounts payable is a liability, a source of finance, albeit a very short-term one, and so we do not need to consider this element of working capital in our determination of transfer prices. Calculating the required return on the investment in accounts receivable is rather a simple matter. Even customers within our organizational family take their time to pay, usually at regular intervals of say every 15 or 30 days. When developing a transfer price, we can presume they will continue to do the same and so we can include in the calculation of our transfer price an allowance for the investment in that particular receivable. Inventory is a different matter however. Quite often, items of inventory are used across a spectrum of products and services and so we need to use an allocation method similar to that for PPE in deciding how much needs to be included in a transfer price for the required return on this asset.

So far, so good. We now know how we shall handle the return on investment in those financial and physical assets that contribute to a transfer pricing transaction. It's time to move on to the considerably more complex situation that applies to each of the four categories of intellectual assets—human capital, structural capital, customer capital, and economic web capital.

Intellectual Assets: Human Capital

It would be sensible to start by understanding what comprises our investment in human capital. The human capital of an organization is made up of the knowledge, skills, competencies, and experiences of those people who are working for the organization. But not all these personal assets and not all employees count as human capital. Only those individuals whose capabilities can be used and incorporated into value-creating processes should be considered as part of the organization's human capital. The remaining employees, whose skills and competencies are readily available in the labor market in equal form, are still valuable to the organization but they are a human resource and not human capital because they don't especially contribute to making a difference in the market. Therefore, the first task is to identify those employees whose individual capabilities contribute to our organization's value-creation system, or business model, to decide whether they should be incorporated into the determination of a value for our human capital.[1]

The first step in establishing a value for the human capital embodied in an organization is to understand the composition of each contributing person's explicit, or domain, knowledge. Despite individuals being significant sources, conduits, and generators of knowledge, the quantum of human capital is not simply the aggregate of each individual employee's domain knowledge. We also have to recognize that additional human capital is created by means of social interaction. This interaction converts the domain knowledge of individuals into collective implicit organizational knowledge, which has a more permanent dimension on which a sustainable competitive advantage may be built. The second step, then, is to assess the quantum of implicit knowledge for the organization that derives from those individuals who are considered to be part of human capital. Combining both of these measures will provide us with a value on which we shall be able to determine the required return that we can build into our transfer pricing activity.

The value of human capital that we shall use in the process of deriving transfer prices stems from a cost-based measurement system and this is preferred for two reasons. First, the value of something is normally at least equal to the amount one is prepared to pay for it. This amount will change from time to time and the basis of valuation should reflect these changes. Second, once the required cost information has been established, it may be applied in all organizations irrespective of their structure, size, and nature of operations. It seems that this approach would provide the best outcome as it produces a more generic model to determine the value of human capital. Furthermore, it is important to bear in mind that the more sophisticated the model, the more expensive it will be to apply, and attempting to achieve a greater degree of precision is not only unnecessary but also may not prove to be cost effective. The aim here is to provide a practical measure, for which the required inputs may be obtained at a reasonable cost, in order to ensure that the importance of human capital will not be neglected in the process of determining transfer prices. Let's start with a way to value domain knowledge.

Domain knowledge comprises both formal and postsecondary education, each of which is exclusive of the other. Since a cost-based measurement system has been proposed as the basis of the valuation of organizational knowledge, we shall start by using the costs associated with attaining a particular level of education as the basis for establishing a pragmatic value of knowledge. Because education is acquired over a period of years, the annual costs will vary. To overcome these variations, we propose using a standard cost based on the most current information. The capitalized value of those costs is proposed as a surrogate measure for the value of the knowledge acquired from a particular level of education. This may be calculated using the formula:

$$K = c\left(\frac{(1+r)^n - 1}{r}\right)$$

where: K = the value of knowledge
c = the standard cost of acquiring knowledge in each time period
r = a long-run rate of return on investment
n = the number of years of education

The cost of acquiring knowledge[2] varies depending on the type of education and it is important to include both the visible cost, irrespective of who pays it, and the opportunity cost in shaping an overall standard cost for each element of domain knowledge. Also, in the valuation model proposed, one important factor that needs to be acquired and used is the long-run rate of return on an investment over time. This, of course, will vary over time and between countries providing an inherent source of comparative advantage in the valuation of human capital. Using the proposed formula, the value for each individual, who is to be considered as part of our organization's human capital, of both their formal education and their postsecondary education may be calculated.

Like most other assets, the benefit of domain knowledge diminishes over time though the nature and rate of depletion may be expected to vary for different types of knowledge. Since a formal education is intended to provide the recipient with lifetime skills, its benefits may reasonably be expected to remain with an individual forever. Yet, from an organization's point of view, the benefit of knowledge acquired from that formal education, though not diminishing in what it provides year-on-year, is only available for the employment period of each individual. In the case of a school-leaver who joins immediately on leaving school, the organization could look forward to the possibility of benefiting from the knowledge acquired from that education for about 50 years. Since the domain knowledge attributable to a person of that standing is expected to be of equal benefit to the organization in each of those 50 years, it may be considered equivalent to the organization acquiring an annuity for each of those years. After a year's employment, and ignoring, for the moment, the impact of inflation, the value of that employee's knowledge to the organization would be the present value of that annuity for 49 years. That is, the depletion for the first year is the present value of the annuity receivable in the 50th year. Depletion of this form of knowledge continues in this way for as long as the person is working for the organization.

The more professionally oriented postsecondary education is treated differently. For this form of knowledge, there is, in addition to the aforementioned, an element of obsolescence. Instead of simply depleting the value of knowledge acquired by the organization over the potential period of employment, it ought to be depleted over the length of time it is expected to provide a benefit to the organization. This will vary depending on the nature of the education. Some forms of knowledge may indeed provide a benefit over the potential period of employment. Others may only provide a benefit during the time a person occupies a certain position in the organization or, indeed, even a function of the expected state of technology. Clearly, because of the diversity of knowledge gained in this way, the most appropriate number of years over which to write off these types of knowledge is likely to differ not only for different types of programs but also for different organizations and different jobs within organizations. What is required is a method, as simple as is reasonably consistent with reality, which takes into account the shorter period that an organization will benefit from this form of knowledge and the value of money over time. It goes without saying that there is no commonality here between organizations and so they have to decide on the most appropriate method for them.

In terms of valuing human capital, this now only leaves us with the task of valuing the implicit knowledge of those employees who are considered part of the value-creating process. Earlier, I suggested that implicit knowledge is created and enlarged by converting, by means of social interaction, the domain knowledge of individuals within the organization. Unfortunately, this form of synergy is difficult to measure. Nevertheless, we must try. So let's start with the notion that implicit knowledge is acquired through social interaction, or the sharing of employee experience. As such, the only cost relevant to the organization is the cost of labor for the time spent by its employees in this way. Here we need to start by understanding how much time is spent by employees during the working day in sharing their knowledge, intentionally or otherwise. No records providing such information are likely to exist and so securing an answer requires a rational assessment that will center on the question of what may be considered reasonable—10%, 15%, or 20%? Undoubtedly, it will vary from one organization to another but, more importantly, it will almost certainly differ between individual employees within an organization and so providing an answer requires careful thought.

Even though employees may spend a regular amount of time throughout their working lives sharing knowledge, the acquisition of implicit knowledge does not have to follow the same path. During the first few years of employment, implicit knowledge would accrue at a slower rate than would normally be expected while the new employee tries to understand what is important. It is also likely that in the latter years of an employee's working life, the acquisition of implicit knowledge would also slow as a degree of disinterest settles in. A similar pattern is found in the classic estimating and forecasting logistic curve, or S-curve. Implicit in S-curve forecasting are assumptions of slow initial growth, subsequent rapid growth followed by declining growth as saturation levels are achieved. This is so similar to the pattern of growth in implicit knowledge that this particular model should be used to determine the expected value of implicit knowledge resident in an individual based on his or her years of service. From this point, the value of an organization's implicit knowledge may be determined very easily. First, from the cohort of value-creating employees, identify for each of them the number of years of service and determine the cumulative value of implicit knowledge attributable to them. Second, aggregate all of these values and the result should provide a reasonable indication of the value of implicit knowledge resident within the organization. Of course, aggregation is not always necessary if you wish the transfer pricing calculation to focus on the value-creating power of individual employees.

From this point, it is simply a matter of adding the two values, that is, for domain and implicit knowledge, for an individual employee to understand the human capital value to the organization of that employee. By applying the required rate of return to that value, you now have an amount that can be included, in the right proportion, into the transfer pricing calculation.

Intellectual Assets: Structural Capital

As before, it would be a good idea to be clear about what we consider to be our investment in structural capital. Put simply, structural capital is the knowledge that gets captured and institutionalized in an organization. It encompasses many things, particularly those that can be patented, copyrighted, or shielded from competitors by other laws. Some examples in this category include technologies, inventions, publications, designs, and processes. Alternatively, we can think about organizational routines and procedures, structures and systems, as well as strategy and culture. This second group is often far more extensive and valuable than the first, which comprises primarily the codified elements of structural capital.

For almost all of these constituents of structural capital, it is possible to treat them in a similar way to PPE when it comes to understanding what to include in the determination of transfer prices. The key is having some record of the costs associated with acquiring or developing individual assets falling into this category. For example, it should be possible to identify the cost of developing a design or invention. Similarly, understanding the cost of putting organizational structures and systems in place makes it easier to incorporate a return on such an investment in our transfer pricing activity.

If we know how much of these assets are used in each transfer pricing activity in relation to the total amount, then we can use the same ratio to determine how much of the required return on any given asset needs to be allocated to each transfer-price calculation.

Intellectual Assets: Customer Capital

Continuing with the concept used already, what do we mean by customer capital? Well, here we are talking about the value of an organization's relationships with its customers, which involve factors such as market share, customer-retention rates, and profitability of customers. In many respects, this is an irrelevant aspect of transfer pricing because we are dealing not with an external customer, but a member of our organizational family. However, our internal customer will be dealing with an external customer and they will leverage their external pricing on the extent of their customer capital. As an upstream member of our family member's value chain, should we not be entitled to some share of their return on customer capital? After all, as you will see from the next section, we shall certainly look to being rewarded for our investment in economic web capital, which is primarily an upstream relationship.

Whether or not to include some return on this particular asset in our intra-family pricing is a strategic decision that will be taken by the organization's senior executives, or even the Board of Directors. If the decision is that it should be included, the calculation is not an exceptionally difficult one. First, we need to determine the quantum of the asset. We do this by calculating the present value of future earnings per customer. After that, it is simply a matter of calculating the return required from the customer overall and allocating some portion of that to an individual transfer price based on the total value of sales to that customer.

Intellectual Assets: Economic Web Capital

This is not much different from customer capital but the focus is very much on the upstream side of the value chain. Our world is changing very quickly and that creates a whole new set of challenges for every organization. Incorporating new technology and dealing with rising customer expectations have forced organizations into the realization that they must rely more heavily on partners and alliances, their economic web.[3] These relationships allow individual members to concentrate on what they do best so that the end result, in the form of the total profitability of all of the members, is a much better one, creating more value for all members of the economic web as well as representing a market-entry hurdle for competitors.

Since the purpose of these economic webs is to enhance an organization's future earning potential, they represent an important asset on which appropriate returns should be secured through the transfer pricing mechanism. Just how we should do that follows the same logic as we applied to customer capital. First, we need to determine the quantum of the asset. We do this by calculating the present value of expected additional future earnings as a result of our membership of a particular economic web. We may, of course, be members of more than one economic web and so the capital value of each needs to be calculated separately. After that, it is simply a matter of calculating the return required from each economic web overall and allocating some portion of that to an individual transfer price based on the total inputs from that web into the product or service that is the subject of the transfer price.

Summary

There is certainly much to consider when it comes to determining transfer prices. What's more, it does sound rather complicated and the product of many different calculations. Fortunately, thanks to the advancements in technology, it is not as difficult as it sounds. The hard part is designing a transfer pricing model best suited to your organization. Once completed, you will then need to know what data are required to properly implement the model. If you look, I'm sure you'll find that much of the input data are readily available in your organization but not in one place. Getting it there is the first task we need to set ourselves if we want to have a transparent and verifiable transfer pricing system. The next task is to actually build the model we have designed for ourselves. For this part of the process, I'll point the way a little in the next chapter by creating an example based on a hypothetical set of circumstances. Finally, we need to translate our model into bits and bytes so that the laborious number crunching is carried out speedily, efficiently, and effectively by a computer.

Obviously, the complexity of the transfer pricing model will depend not only on the size of our organization but also on the number of intra-family transactions and interventions that require the establishment of a transfer price. That said, why limit application of the model developed for transfer pricing just to those intra-family activities? Why not treat it as a pricing model more generally and use it to set prices in those situations where you are not driven by market forces? Finally, even for those sales where market conditions determine your selling price, why not use it as a management tool to evaluate whether you really should be selling those products or services to that customer at those prices?

CHAPTER 6

A Practical Example

Introduction

So far I've had plenty to say in relation to the rise in importance of transfer pricing—how trade has grown over time, how the need for transfer pricing came about, the difficulties that MNEs and transnationals encounter along the way, and the things that every organizational family needs to think about when it is creating its own transfer pricing system. It is not an easy task and I'd have a small wager that a reader out there somewhere will think of something I have forgotten. Now it's time to move on and give you a practical example that you may be able to relate to, or that will give you a foundation for developing your own model.

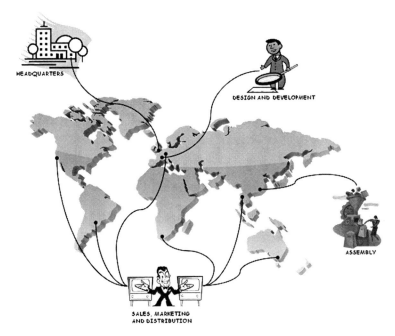

Figure 6.1. The Penny Farthing plc organizational family.

Headquarters	HQ
Design and development	DD
Assembly	AY
Sales, marketing and distribution:	
Africa	BU1
Asia	BU2
Australia and the Pacific	BU3
Europe and the Middle East	BU4
North America	BU5
South America	BU6

Here I'm going to work with a fictitious organizational family that is headed up by a British public company that I have called *Penny Farthing plc*. I'm sure you can all guess what they will be doing. Yes, that's it—they will be designing, assembling but not manufacturing as all of the component parts will be made by their upstream business partners—their economic web, and selling bicycles. Figure 6.1 provides an overview of what they are doing where. From this picture, I shall document the hypothetical cost and asset structures of each of the business units as well as the interventions between them. After that, the relevant transfer prices will be established. Finally, I'll test the model to see whether, as a result of applying this transfer pricing model, Penny Farthing plc is creating additional economic value for its owners.

Let's start by documenting the cost and asset structures of each member of the organizational family to whom I shall allocate the following acronyms to make it easier to follow:

Building a Transfer Price

Starting at the top of the tree with the organization's HQ, which is based in the United Kingdom, there are four functional areas that we need to examine: strategic management, knowledge management, financial management, and legal services. Each of these has employees, some expenses, and an asset base that needs to be taken into consideration when determining the amount of management fee that will be passed on to every other unit in the organizational family in the form of a monthly or quarterly management fee.

The strategic management function provides advice and support in the establishment of business plans as well as conducting regular performance reviews with each of the member organizations in the organizational family. The knowledge management function focuses on human resource management as well as attending to all of the information technology needs of the organizational family. Data are processed in the cloud and performance reporting is online, real-time at each unit. The financial management function is responsible for negotiating for the financial requirements of the group and the preparation of statutory financial reporting for all units. In addition, it assumes responsibility for overall risk management, including the treasury function. Finally, legal services provide advice on legal issues arising anywhere in the world and are responsible for tax planning and the submission of all the necessary documentation with regard to tax matters in every jurisdiction. These activities form the basis of determining the annual HQ charge.

Figure 6.2 provides a summary of the calculations that are made to determine the management fee that will be charged and nominates the basis of making that charge to the other units in the family. Utilizing the basis of

HEADQUARTERS					
	Strategy	Knowledge	Financial	Legal	Common
Capital base					
Financial assets	0	0	0	25,000	
Physical assets	27,000	86,000	36,000	18,000	
Intellectual assets					
- human capital	359,200	158,700	192,500	169,000	
- structural capital	12,400	76,500	30,700	18,600	
- customer capital	0	0	0	0	
- economic web capital	0	83,300	70,800	166,700	
	398,600	404,500	330,000	397,300	
Costs					
Salaries and benefits	385,000	350,000	390,000	235,000	
Facilities	30,000	50,000	40,000	20,000	140,000
Depreciation	2,700	13,600	3,600	1,800	
Other supplies	7,500	25,000	10,000	5,000	
Contracted services	0	12,000	65,000	20,000	
	425,200	450,600	508,600	281,800	
Return on capital at 12%	47,800	48,500	39,600	47,700	
	473,000	499,100	548,200	329,500	
Basis of charge	Unit	Employee	Transactions	Unit	

Figure 6.2. Headquarters capital base and costs.

DD	£118,000
AY	£825,600
BU1	£148,400
BU2	£187,300
BU3	£125,700
BU4	£139,100
BU5	£157,300
BU6	£148,400

apportionment shown for each of the four functional areas, the annual HQ charge for each member of the family would be:

The next member of the organizational family that we shall look at is the DD team, which is based in Switzerland. Perhaps, the most significant difference here is the amount of structural capital that exists in this area as a result of design patents and development improvements as well as the detailed instructions that are provided to the AY division to ensure the quality of the final product.

We also need to remember that the HQ charge that is incorporated into this cost structure is in Pounds Sterling and needs to be converted into Swiss Francs. This process is managed by the financial management team at HQ and the cost of doing it is built into the HQ annual charge.

Figure 6.3 provides a summary of the calculations that are made to determine the amount to be recovered and nominates the basis of making that charge to the other units in the family. Utilizing the basis of apportionment shown for each of the two functional areas, and assuming that the development cost will be recovered entirely from the AY unit, which in turn will pass this along to the individual business units, the annual DD charge for each member of the family would be:

AY	CHF 507,600
BU1 (1 model)	CHF 48,400
BU2 (2 models)	CHF 96,800
BU3 (2 models)	CHF 96,800
BU4 (3 models)	CHF 145,300
BU5 (3 models)	CHF 145,300
BU6 (1 model)	CHF 48,400

DESIGN AND DEVELOPMENT		
	Design	Development
Capital base		
Financial assets	0	0
Physical assets	46,500	86,000
Intellectual assets		
- human capital	421,200	487,800
- structural capital	120,900	31,700
- customer capital	0	0
- economic web capital	0	0
	588,600	605,500
Costs		
Salaries and benefits	328,000	286,000
Facilities	45,000	45,000
Depreciation and amortization	10,700	10,200
Other supplies	10,500	5,000
Contracted services	27,500	0
Headquarters charge	88,700	88,700
	510,400	434,900
Return on capital at 12%	70,600	72,700
	581,000	507,600
Basis of charge	Number of models	Units produced

Figure 6.3. Design and development capital base and costs.

As we progress through the organizational family in the construction of our relevant transfer prices, we come to the end of the chain, which is the AY division based in Hong Kong. From here, the bicycles, of which there are four different models, are delivered to the six business units that are the Sales, Marketing, and Distribution outlets. From there, they are sold to independent retailers at various prices depending on what the local markets will bear. So, let's focus on the AY function. Apart from collecting the charges from HQ and DD, the AY function has its own costs and capital base to consider. Perhaps, the most important difference here is the large amount of economic web capital. This arises because all of the component parts, including painted frames, are bought in from a network of suppliers located around the world. Also, most of its workforce is only considered to be human resources as they could be replaced very easily with equally suitable employees. Even so, there are a number of employees here who are treated as human capital because their knowledge of AY procedures, the various business divisions' requirements, and management skills are highly valued.

Figure 6.4 provides a summary of the cost to produce one of each of the four models of bicycles and, as such, represents the FOB (free on board) selling price to all of the six business units that are the Sales, Marketing, and Distribution outlets. Individually, they will have different shipping costs, import tariffs, and operating costs of their own associated with the receipt and sale of the bicycles that need to be taken into

ASSEMBLY				
	Model 1	Model 2	Model 3	Model 4
Capital base				
Financial assets	0	0	0	0
Physical assets	7,054,300	842,300	912,500	342,200
Intellectual assets				
- human capital	34,107,200	4,072,500	4,411,900	1,527,200
- structural capital	833,300	109,400	124,000	46,600
- customer capital	0	0	0	0
- economic web capital	28,237,200	4,213,800	5,919,600	2,848,200
	70,232,000	9,238,000	11,368,000	4,764,200
Costs				
Components	67,769,200	8,427,600	10,147,800	3,797,600
Salaries and benefits	52,472,600	6,265,400	6,787,500	2,349,500
Facilities	1,159,600	138,500	150,000	51,900
Depreciation	705,400	84,200	91,300	34,200
Other supplies	3,388,500	488,700	822,800	542,500
Headquarters charge	7,978,200	952,600	1,032,000	357,200
Design and development charge	3,296,300	393,600	426,400	147,600
	136,769,800	16,750,600	19,457,800	7,280,500
Return on capital at 12%	8,427,800	1,108,600	1,364,200	571,700
	145,197,600	17,859,200	20,822,000	7,852,200
Basis of charge per unit (HK$)	481.60	496.10	533.90	581.60
Basis of charge per unit (US$)	62.10	64.00	68.90	75.10

Figure 6.4. Assembly capital base, costs, and free-on-board selling prices.

account when deciding if they are able to make an adequate return for Penny Farthing plc overall. Although this last part is not a transfer pricing activity, it is essential to understand the whole picture. For now, we need to understand, using the more traditional measures of performance, whether building transfer prices in this way produces a positive result for the organization.

Evaluating the Result

The first task in our evaluation is to look at the data that have been used in this example and restate it in more traditional terms. Figure 6.5 does that and expresses the outcome in just one currency, that of the home of Penny Farthing plc's HQ, The United Kingdom.

Even without the operating profit generated by the final sale of the bicycles, the traditional performance measures suggest that a reasonable return is being made by the organization for all of those functions that

PENNY FARTHING plc				
	Headquarters	Design and development	Assembly	Total
Capital base				
Financial assets	25,000	0	0	25,000
Physical assets	167,000	88,300	732,100	987,400
	192,000	88,300	732,100	1,012,400
Revenues				
Sale of bicycles to business units	0	0	15,338,900	15,338,900
Charges to business units	906,200	387,300	0	1,293,500
	906,200	387,300	15,338,900	16,632,400
Costs				
Components	0	0	7,211,400	7,211,400
Salaries and benefits	1,360,000	409,300	5,430,000	7,199,300
Facilities	140,000	60,000	120,000	320,000
Depreciation	21,700	13,900	73,200	108,800
Other supplies	47,500	10,300	419,400	477,200
Contracted services	97,000	18,300	0	115,300
	1,666,200	511,800	13,254,000	15,432,000
Operating profit	(760,000)	(124,500)	2,084,900	1,200,400
Return on sales				7.8%
Return on capital employed				118.6%

Figure 6.5. Traditional performance measurement of Penny Farthing plc.

are essentially driven by a transfer pricing mechanism. Nowhere, in any of our calculations to this point, was a profit requirement, perhaps the most contentious element of transfer pricing, used. While there will no doubt be debate surrounding the determination of the capital base on which the required return on capital is calculated, perhaps this model of determining transfer prices will find acceptance in the economic times in which we live.

Finally, to complete the task that I set out to achieve, that is whether the transfer pricing model creates additional economic value for the owners of Penny Farthing plc, we return to the use of EVA®. Applying an average tax rate of 25% to the total operating profit, this transfer pricing model shows that we are creating the additional value added that is the fundamental objective of transfer pricing. Here is the calculation to support that statement:

$$EVA® = Net\ operating\ profit\ after\ tax - (WACC \times capital\ invested)$$
$$= (1,200,400 \times 0.75) - (0.12 \times 1,012,400)$$
$$= 900,300 - 121,488$$
$$= 778,812$$

Summary

I said in my preface to this book that any transfer pricing model should focus on managerial issues and in particular as a driver to add value throughout the organization. The model that I have presented to you in this chapter, which is based on the foundation that was developed throughout the book, has done just that. It will not be everyone's ideal solution but it provides a starting point for discussion and further development.

No doubt many of you will be bewildered by the calculations that have to take place to arrive at an effective transfer price using this model. Fear not for, as long as you have the data available, an experienced user of enterprise resource planning (ERP) systems will be able to generate the necessary calculations from those data so that you will have access to an instantaneous transfer price for any product or service that you offer within your organizational family. If your organization is not big enough to run an ERP system, someone more proficient than me with an Excel spreadsheet will be able to build one for you as long as you are able to give them the underlying parameters.

This is achievable with thought but I'd imagine that the biggest task of all will be getting all of the data that's needed in one accessible place. I can safely say it's a task that needs to be done for you and will benefit considerably in the long run from doing so. Good luck with constructing your transfer pricing model!

Epilogue

As the commercial world continues its exponential rate of change, every organization looks to find ways that will satisfy the insatiable appetite of financial markets for continuous growth. To this end, FDI plays an extraordinary and growing role in global business. It may provide an enterprise with new markets and marketing channels, cheaper production facilities, and access to new technology, products, skills, and financing. For a host country, or the foreign enterprise that receives the investment, FDI may provide a source of new technologies, capital, processes, products, organizational technologies, and management skills and, as such, is able to provide a strong impetus to economic development.

In the past decade, FDI has come to play a major role in the internationalization of business. Reacting to changes in technology, growing liberalization of the national regulatory framework governing investment in enterprises, and changes in capital markets, profound changes have occurred in the size, scope, and methods of FDI. New information technology systems, and the decline in global communication costs, have made the management of foreign investments far easier than in the past. Furthermore, the sea change during the same period of time in trade and investment policies and the global regulatory environment, including trade policy and tariff liberalization, easing of restrictions on foreign investment and acquisition in many nations, and the deregulation and privatization of many industries, has probably been the most significant catalyst for FDI's expanded role.

For small- and medium-sized companies, FDI represents an opportunity to become more actively involved in international business activities, which, in the fullness of time, will inevitably lead to an active involvement in transfer-pricing activities. No doubt many of you will consider it premature to be thinking of things that don't apply in the present. You may be right, but when you are making substantial investments in knowledge-management activities within your organization, thinking about the possibilities that the future will bring is a critical part of the planning process. Nowhere is this more apparent than in the design of management systems that are intended to bring transparency to business processes and relationships.

The aim of this book was to provide, which I trust I have done, new thinking of how we determine the price of goods and services exchanged between economic units belonging to the same organizational family— one that will reduce friction and conflict between all of the interested factions. Of course, nothing may ever be considered all encompassing and this surely also applies to what I have written in this book. The ideas and concepts are mine, and mine alone, so there is every possibility that they could be improved upon. I can only hope that the model I have described will act as a catalyst in many organizations for thinking about a more comprehensive way of ensuring that their transfer prices more accurately reflect the drivers of economic wealth in each and all of their many functional areas.

We have now come to the end of this book. I hope you have enjoyed reading it and that, in some way, it will provide you with some good ideas for your organization. But, to quote a statesman[1] from an earlier era: "Now this is not the end. It is not even the beginning of the end. But it is, perhaps, the end of the beginning."

Thank you so much!

Notes

Chapter 1

1. *The Land of Punt*, described in the chronicles of ancient Egypt, is somewhat of a mystery for we remain uncertain of its exact location. It is generally considered to be located in the regions of Djibouti, Eritrea, Ethiopia, and the Horn of Africa although many modern Egyptologists place it much closer to Egypt.
2. See chapter 7, entitled *On Free Trade*, in Ricardo (1817).
3. Based on the ratio of merchandise trade (exports and imports combined) to gross domestic product at current prices obtained from the United Nations Statistics Division and the OECD statistical service.
4. An excellent example of this is Elance Inc., which claims to be the world's leading platform for online employment, helping organizations hire and manage in the cloud (see http://www.elance.com).
5. Fukuyama (1992).
6. In Australia, the French chemical giant SNF (Australia) successfully appealed against an Australian Tax Office–imposed penalty for transfer pricing and, in Canada, the Federal Court overturned a tax penalty on a Canadian pharmaceutical company for overpaying a Swiss affiliate for the active ingredient in the ulcer-fighting drug, Zantac.
7. *Transfer Pricing Guidelines for Multinational Enterprises and Tax Administrations* was published by the OECD in August 2010.

Chapter 2

1. Through Amazon.com, an Apple iPod Nano 8GB costs £102 (equivalent to US$160 using January 2012 exchange rates) from their British site and US$120 from their American site.
2. There are many books available that provide an extensive discussion on costing systems. Chapter 3 in my book, *Effective Financial Management: The Cornerstone for Success*, provides an overview of the possibilities suitable in different situations.
3. The founding countries of the Joint International Tax Shelter Information Centre are leading the charge here by increasing the transfer pricing disclosure requirements for organizations that do business with related parties overseas as well as instituting aggressive transfer pricing audits in areas they consider being high risk.

Chapter 3

1. UNCTADstat (November 6, 2011).
2. This excludes the regular double -taxation that occurs at a federal and state level in countries such as the United States.
3. World Bank (2006).
4. www.wcoomd.org/home_valoverviewboxes_valwcoiccpartnership _valwcooecdpartnership.htm, accessed March 2, 2012.

Chapter 4

1. Friedman (2006), p. 459.
2. Friedman (2006), p. 246.
3. Wetlaufer (2001), pp. 112–121.

Chapter 5

1. The dialogue that follows about determining the value of human capital is adapted from Turner and Jackson-Cox (2002), pp. 101–111.
2. In all cases, no distinction is made between the qualities of graduands. While some will always be better than others, the granting of an award assumes a certain level of knowledge common to all.
3. There is plenty of evidence of this with, perhaps, the most recent significant example being the alliance between Emirates and Qantas that will take effect in April 2013.

Epilogue

1. From a speech by Sir Winston Churchill at the Mansion House, London, on November 10, 1942.

References

Friedman, T. L. (2006). *The world is flat: The globalized world in the twenty-first century.* London: Penguin Books Ltd.

Fukuyama, F. (1992). *The end of history and the last man.* New York: Avon Books.

Ricardo, D. (1817). *On the principles of political economy and taxation.* London: John Murray.

Turner, G. (2011). *Effective financial management: The cornerstone for success.* New York: Business Expert Press.

Turner, G., & Jackson-Cox, J. (2002). If management requires measurement, how may we cope with knowledge? *Singapore Management Review 24*(3).

UNCTADstat, *Inward and outward foreign direct investment flows, annual, 1970–2010,* http://unctadstat.unctad.org/TableViewer/tableView.aspx, accessed 6th November 2011.

Wetlaufer, S. (2001). The business case against revolution: An interview with Nestlé's Peter Brabeck. *Harvard Business Review 79*(2).

World Bank (2006). *Paying taxes: The global picture.* Washington, DC: The World Bank.

Index

OTHER TITLES IN THE INTERNATIONAL BUSINESS COLLECTION

Tamer Cavusgil, Georgia State, Michael Czinkota, Georgetown, and Gary Knight, Florida State University, Collection Editors

- *Successful Cross-Cultural Management: A Guide for International Managers* by Parissa Haghirian
- *Inside Washington: Government Resources for International Business, Sixth Edition* by William Delphos
- *Practical Solutions to Global Business Negotiations* by Claude Cellich and Subhash Jain
- *Trade Promotion Strategies: Best Practices* by Claude Cellich and Michel Borgeon
- *As I Was Saying...Observations on International Business and Trade Policy, Exports, Education, and the Future* by Michael Czinkota
- *China: Doing Business in the Middle Kingdom* by Stuart Strother
- *Essential Concepts of Cross-Cultural Management: Building on What We All Share* by Lawrence A. Beer
- *As the World Turns...Observations on International Business and Policy, Going International and Transition* by Michael Czinkota
- *Assessing and Mitigating Business Risks in India* by Balbir Bhasin
- *The Emerging Markets of the Middle East: Strategies for Entry and Growth* by Tim Rogmans
- *Doing Business in China Getting Ready for the Asian Century* by Jane Menzies, Mona Chung, and Stuart Orr

Announcing the Business Expert Press Digital Library

Concise E-books Business Students Need for Classroom and Research

This book can also be purchased in an e-book collection by your library as
- a one-time purchase,
- that is owned forever,
- allows for simultaneous readers,
- has no restrictions on printing, and
- can be downloaded as PDFs from within the library community.

Our digital library collections are a great solution to beat the rising cost of textbooks. e-books can be loaded into their course management systems or onto student's e-book readers.

The **Business Expert Press** digital libraries are very affordable, with no obligation to buy in future years. For more information, please visit **www.businessexpertpress.com/librarians**. To set up a trial in the United States, please contact **Adam Chesler** at *adam.chesler@ businessexpertpress.com* for all other regions, contact **Nicole Lee** at *nicole.lee@igroupnet.com*.

CPSIA information can be obtained at www.ICGtesting.com
Printed in the USA
BVOW011745200513

321184BV00006B/17/P